MW00628263

Sacred Dance
in the
Ancient World

Sacred Dance
in the
Ancient World

W.O.E. Oesterley

DOVER PUBLICATIONS, INC.
Mineola, New York

Bibliographical Note

This Dover edition, first published in 2002, is an unabridged republication of *The Sacred Dance: A Study in Comparative Folklore,* published by Cambridge University Press in 1923.

Library of Congress Cataloging-in-Publication Data

Oesterley, W. O. E. (William Oscar Emil), 1866-1950.
   [Sacred dance]
   Sacred dance in the ancient world / W. O. E. Oesterley.
      p. cm.
   Originally published: The sacred dance. Cambridge : Cambridge University Press, 1923.
   Includes bibliographical references and index.
   ISBN 0-486-42494-4 (pbk.)
      1. Dance—Religious aspects—History. I. Title.

BL605 .04 2002
291.3'7—dc21

2002031296

Manufactured in the United States of America
Dover Publications, Inc., 31 East 2nd Street, Mineola, N.Y. 11501

PREFACE

THE following study is an attempt to estimate the part played by the Sacred Dance among the peoples of antiquity as well as among the uncultured races in modern times; to account for its origin; to note the occasions on which it was performed; and to indicate the purposes of its performance.

The subject is more complicated than would appear at first sight; for while the fact of its universal prevalence among all races at one time or another of their cultural development shows how essential a rite it was, its origin is obviously veiled in obscurity seeing that it developed in pre-historic times. So that in seeking to throw light on the question of its origin one has to try to get at the back of the mind of the savage, and envisage things from his point of view; but that mind represents a complex of such crass and illogical elements that one may easily be led astray.

The purpose of the Sacred Dance, again, presents us with another set of problems; for while in some cases this is clear enough, in others there are alternatives which suggest themselves; and, further, it is probable that a variety of motives not infrequently prompted its performance. To disentangle these is not always easy.

On the other hand, the interest of the subject from the human point of view is great; for, as an indispensable rite at all the crises of life, it was evidently a means of emotional outlet. From the psychological standpoint, therefore, its prevalence is not without importance. Indeed, it will probably be thought that from the psychological side the subject is inadequately treated in the following pages. And this is true, though it does receive some attention; but in extenuation it must be said that the writer's main object has been merely to give some account of the Sacred Dance as a widespread rite; and he feels that its treatment from the psychological aspect would best be left to one who is an expert in psychology.

That the Old Testament figures somewhat prominently in the following pages is partly due to the fact that the writer has made a special study of this body of literature, and it seemed wise to start from that with which he was most conversant; but there is the further reason, as is pointed out in the introductory chapter, that the Old Testament offers, in most cases, an exceedingly convenient starting-point from which to study the various "types" of sacred dance.

The writer desires to express his thanks to Dr Jevons, Dr Lukyn Williams, and Dr S. A. Cook for a number of helpful suggestions, to Miss Bevan for reading through the proofs, and his warm appreciation of the kindness and courtesy of the Secretary of the University Press.

The minute care taken in pointing out oversights in the correction of proofs, as well as other slips, is most gratefully acknowledged.

Finally, the writer would like to take this opportunity of thanking the Curator of the Department of Greek and Roman Antiquities in the British Museum for his ready help in arranging for the photographing of the Greek Vase, representing a Maenad dancing in honour of Dionysos, which is reproduced on the cover of this book.

W. O. E. O.

St Alban's Vicarage,
   Bedford Park.
     February 1923.

CONTENTS

CHAPTER I

INTRODUCTORY

CHAPTER II

THE ORIGIN AND PURPOSES
OF THE SACRED DANCE

CHAPTER III

THE SACRED DANCE AMONG
THE ISRAELITES

CHAPTER IV

THE OLD TESTAMENT TERMS FOR "DANCING"

CHAPTER V

THE SACRED PROCESSIONAL DANCE, AND DANCES IN HONOUR OF SUPERNATURAL POWERS

CHAPTER VI

THE RITUAL DANCE ROUND A SACRED OBJECT

CHAPTER VII

THE ECSTATIC DANCE

CHAPTER VIII

THE SACRED DANCE AT VINTAGE, HARVEST, AND OTHER FESTIVALS

CHAPTER IX

DANCES IN CELEBRATION OF VICTORY

CHAPTER X

THE SACRED DANCE AS A MARRIAGE RITE

CHAPTER XI

DANCING AS A MOURNING AND BURIAL RITE

ABBREVIATIONS

DB. Hastings' *Dictionary of the Bible.*

EB. Cheyne's *Encyclopaedia Biblica.*

ERE. Hastings' *Encyclopaedia of Religion and Ethics.*

GB. Frazer's *The Golden Bough: A Study in Magic and Religion* (3rd edition).

JE. The *Jewish Encyclopaedia.*

CHAPTER I

INTRODUCTORY

I

Our study is concerned with the "sacred" dance; that this epithet applied to the dance, at any rate during the earlier phases of its history and as still practised among many uncultured and even some semi-cultured peoples to-day, is more than justified, the following pages will, it is hoped, show.

Its extreme importance in the eyes of early man, who regarded it as indispensable at all the crises of life—initiation, puberty, marriage, burial—who used it as one of the essentials in worship, who saw in it a means of propitiating whatever supernatural powers he believed in, a means of communion with the deity, a means of obtaining good crops, fruitful marriages, and of communicating with the departed—to mention only its more important uses, shows that it is a subject worth investigating though the domain it occupies is but a modest one in the great sphere of the history of Religion.

Probably one of the most instructive first-hand pieces of information which we have on the subject is contained in the answers given to Chalmers in reply to questions which he addressed to some natives of New Guinea. He asked "*What does the dance signify?*" and he got two replies from the natives of the two most important districts of this big island respectively; the first ran thus:

When they dance all the spirits rejoice, as do all the people. When dancing, all food grows well; but when

not dancing, food grows badly. No drums are beaten
uselessly [the drum-beating is the invariable accompaniment to dancing, one implies the other]. When anyone
dies drums are beaten to comfort friends.

The second was this:

Drum-beating and dancing are a sign of rejoicing and
thanksgiving, in order that by so doing there may be a
large harvest. If the dancing is not given there will be
an end to the good growth; but if it is continued, all
will go well. People come in from other villages and will
dance all night. There will be several feasts during the
time, and each leader of the dance will pray and thank
the spirits for the good harvest.

Among other questions he also asked: "*Is there any
useless dancing?*" and the two replies were: "No, the
drum is never beaten uselessly"; and: "Dances are
never merely useless[1]."

The study of the subject brings out without a shadow
of doubt that these answers illustrate what were, and still
are to a great extent, the beliefs held in regard to the
sacred dance by numbers of peoples in an undeveloped
stage of culture. It is a good illustration of what, within
a circumscribed area, holds good of the wider study of
religions in general, that, as Farnell has so well put it,

all through the present societies of savage men there
prevails an extraordinary uniformity, in spite of much
local variation, in ritual and mythology, a uniformity
so striking as to suggest belief in an ultimately identical
tradition, or, perhaps more reasonably, the psychologic
theory that the human brain-cell in different races at
the same stage of development responds with the same

[1] *Pioneering in New Guinea*, pp. 181 f. (1887); see further,
J. E. Harrison, *Ancient Art and Ritual*, pp. 31 ff. (1913).

religious speech or the same religious act to the same *stimuli* supplied by its environment[1].

A survey over the whole field produces the conviction that the *stimuli* which, in its beginnings, induced the sacred dance appear to have been what we should now describe as the two prime spiritual and material needs, respectively, of man, viz. the response to his "god," and the obtaining of food. To early savage man it was not, of course, a god as we understand the word, nor yet even as it would have been understood for millenniums among uncivilized men in remote ages; we merely use the word as a convenient term for expressing a supernatural power, or powers, at first vague, impersonal, "mana[2]," or something of that kind; at any rate, some power beyond the ken of man, of whose existence he had no doubt whatsoever, and to which he was impelled to respond to the best of his very feeble powers. Why he should have chosen this form of response (we are not contending that it was the only form) is a difficult, perhaps an impossible, question to answer, though we shall make the attempt to do so (see pp. 15 ff.); but that he did choose this form all the available evidence goes to show. That the sacred dance should have been believed to be the means of obtaining food is less difficult to understand when one remembers the universal belief in the efficacy of imitative magic among uncivilized men. The natives of New Guinea dance as a means of obtaining a good harvest; but there is evidence for the presumption that early man did the same thing for obtaining food long before harvests existed.

[1] *The Evolution of Religion*, p. 9 (1905); cp. the same author's *Greece and Babylon*, p. 37 (1911).
[2] See Marett, *The Threshold of Religion*, pp. 128 ff. (1909).

As a means of response to supernatural powers the dance was obviously a sacred act; but the epithet may also be applied, though perhaps in a modified way, to the dance as a means of obtaining food; for the belief in the existence of supernatural powers once attained, the conviction of their intrusion into all the affairs of life would naturally follow, as indeed we know to have been the case. But this implies that savage man believed that these supernatural powers were, in some sense, the givers of food; and this is hardly compatible with the idea that the dance as an act of imitative magic was the means of procuring food—an idea which is abundantly proved by the evidence to exist. If an act of imitative magic, such as the dance, is *ipso facto* the means of bringing out what it imitates, how can it be said that supernatural powers have anything to do with the matter? And how can the dance in this case be called sacred? It is a question, however, whether there was not a subconscious intention of setting in motion the "machinery" which brought about the thing imitated every time an act of imitative magic was performed. By the "machinery" we mean the active intervention of supernatural powers in an undefined, mysterious way. In this case the dance as a means of obtaining food would likewise be, strictly speaking, a sacred act.

However this may be, there is a large consensus of opinion that the dance in its origin was sacred, and that every other subsequent form of dance was ultimately derived from this. It is true to say that "the ritual or worship dance is the source of all others[1]." One of the

[1] Mrs Lilly Grove (now Lady Frazer) and other writers, *Dancing*, p. 8 (1895); elsewhere in the same volume the writers say: "There must have been a period of the world's history when every action in life, every game, every banquet, every dance, was a game, a repast, a dance, in honour of the gods," p. 15. The evidence

earliest modern writers on the subject, de Cahusac, likewise says: "Aussi la danse sacrée est-elle la plus ancienne,
et la source dans laquelle on a puisé dans les suites toutes
les autres[1]." This point is particularly emphasized
because it is only the dance in its *sacred* aspect that
will be dealt with in the following pages.

II

As soon as one attempts to define what dancing in its
essence is one realizes the difficulty of doing so. It can
be defined in such a number of ways, all of which contain
elements of truth; so much depends upon the point of
view taken in regard to it. The recording of a number
of definitions would be wearisome, Voss alone gives
dozens by different people[2]. But one thing which these
various definitions teach must be noted and insisted
upon: they show that the term "dancing" connotes a
great deal more than is attached to it now-a-days. When,
for example, de Cahusac rightly defines dancing as "l'art
des gestes[3]," it is obvious that these cannot be restricted
to the feet or legs. A number of the Egyptian inscriptions make it clear that the arms played as important
a part in the dance as the legs; representations of it on
Greek pottery show that the motions of the head, and
even more of the whole body, are necessary parts in the
movements of the dance; among some savages the sacred

entirely bears this out if we take "gods" as meaning supernatural
powers in general.

[1] *La danse ancienne et moderne, ou Traité Historique de la Danse,*
p. 19 (1754). For a different opinion see Irving King, *The
Development of Religion,* p. 58 (1910).

[2] *Der Tanz und seine Geschichte,* pp. 3–15 (1869).

[3] He says: "Les différentes affections de l'âme sont donc
l'origine des gestes, et la danse qui en est composée, est par consé-
quent l'art de les faire avec grâce et mesure relativement aux
affections qu'ils doivent exprimer," *op. cit.* p. 17.

dance is performed while the legs are more or less still, but the arms and the body are constantly in motion. To make but one reference to modern dancing: in some of the figures of the quadrille the dancers simply advance and recede, and at times they are stationary, merely bowing; yet this all belongs to the dance, and comes under the category of dancing. Crawley truly says that "dancing is an instinctive mode of muscular expression of feeling[1]." If, then, the feelings are restrained the muscular expression may take the form of a staid procession, as seems to be characteristic of the Assyrian sacred dance. We must, therefore, include under the many forms of the sacred dance such as range from a formal procession, stately and measured, to those of the wild orgy in the Dionysiac ritual. As we shall see, the *intention* which prompts the dance will have a great deal to do with its external form; a fact which gives point to Giraudet's phrase that "la danse a été l'expression d'un état d'âme[2]."

The wide connotation which must be accorded to the word "dancing" is illustrated by what the Bedouin Arabs understand by it. They are a race which, as is well known, has retained many beliefs, customs, and practices which have been handed down from time immemorial; therefore the evidence afforded by them is valuable. By dance, which they call *raḳṣ*, they understand every rhythmic movement of hands or feet, whether remaining on the same spot or not[3]. Of them

[1] *ERE*, x. 358 a.

[2] *Traité de la Danse*, p. 8 (1891). Jevons (in a private communication) lays much stress on the sacred dance being, like every rite, "an expression of will."

[3] See Dalman, *Palestinischer Diwan*, p. 254 (1901); cp. Harrison, *op. cit.* p. 31.

as of all other peoples rhythm is as inseparable from the movements of the dance "as it is from other bodily functions, and therefore belongs to it without saying[1]"; but, as the Arabs show, rhythmic movements can be performed while standing on one spot; emotions can be expressed by the rhythmic movements of the arms and of the body and of the head while the legs may be more or less motionless.

"The human instinct of play," says Crawley, "is closely connected with the human love of excitement. The dance satisfies both, and its rhythmical character also makes it suitable for the expression of the most solemn and controlled emotions. It is at once the servant of Apollo and of Dionysus[2]."

The close, one may almost say the inseparable, connexion between the dance and music is as marked in its sacred as in its secular character. In the first instance it is the rhythmic instinct which demands this, so that among many savages the "music" which accompanies the dance is the mere clapping of hands, or the striking together of pieces of wood, or the beating of the tom-tom, all in rhythmical time. The same is also found among some peoples more advanced on the path of culture, though they usually add the sound of other instruments, among which the flute figures prominently. Singing is, of course, and always has been, another favourite accompaniment to the dance. The Bedouin Arabs accompany their dances by the beating of cymbals or of hand-drums, or by clapping of hands; sometimes singing accompanies the dancing[3]. This was also the case among the Israelites.

---

[1] Crawley, *ERE*, x. 358 *a*.
[2] *Ibid*. See further Toy, *Intr. to the Hist. of Religions*, p. 50 (1913).   [3] Dalman, *op. cit.* pp. 254 f.

III

In the following discussion on the sacred dance we have made the Old Testament our starting-point. In spite of some drawbacks which will become very apparent, this course has its advantages. The Old Testament offers, either explicitly or implicitly, as we hope to show, evidence of the existence among the ancient Israelites of most of the typical sacred dances of antiquity. By "typical" we do not mean dances in their outward form, but in the intention and object for which they were performed. In dealing with sacred dances it is only by considering their intention and purpose that a classification of them can be attempted. The Old Testament gives within the compass of its pages certain *points d'appui* which afford convenient starting-points for the consideration of these different types of the sacred dance. Then, in each case we go on to the further investigation of these among various other races. From this we are often able to discern, with tolerable probability, the early underlying ideas which prompted the performance of the type of dance in question; for, as may well be supposed, it is not from the Israelites that we can expect to discover, excepting in the one case of the ecstatic dance, the root motives of the different types of the sacred dance. The most promising sphere for the discernment of these is among the uncivilized races; their *naïve* and unsophisticated naturalness reveals things which a gradually developing civilization obscures. Hence the devoting of a good deal of attention to the sacred dance among savages in the following pages.

Another advantage of using the Old Testament for our various starting-points is that the Israelites were in that stage of culture in which a people still retains many more or less primitive rites and customs while pushing forward on the path of cultural development; so that among them we are in touch with the past and yet experiencing the upward trend that is taking place. Crawley truly says that "it is in the middle stages of culture that dancing is seen at its highest development[1]"; that applies to the Israelites. It is like standing on an eminence and looking behind and before. That has its advantages. At the same time, we are not blind to the drawbacks involved. For in some important instances the Old Testament is silent. We give reasons which we believe are sufficient to explain this silence. But when a particular type of the sacred dance is not mentioned in the Old Testament it must not be supposed that it did not exist; indirect evidence is forthcoming which makes it highly probable that the reverse is the case. For this reason we shall often refer to post-biblical Jewish custom and practice. Such a thing as the sacred dance is not likely, from the very nature of things, to have been an innovation of later ages; so that its existence in post-biblical times may well be regarded as the continuance of traditional custom; and if so, its existence among the Israelites of Old Testament times may be taken for granted.

Still, we realize the precariousness of seeming, in some cases, to build upon an apparently non-existing foundation; but the risk must be taken, and, as we hope to show, the evidence from subsequent times justifies the risk.

IV

A few words must be said about the sources from which information regarding the sacred dance is to be gained.

[1] *ERE*, x. 358 *a*.

(1) There are a certain number of ancient inscriptions of various kinds upon which dancing is represented. On these the dancing is not always of a religious character; but it is not difficult to discern when it is religious and when secular. For example, there is a very valuable fragment of an Egyptian fresco belonging to the 18th dynasty (B.C. 1600–1450) in the British Museum[1], on which two nude women dancers are depicted; the dancing is accompanied by other women, some clapping their hands, and others playing the flute. But another part of the fresco shows clearly enough that the scene represents a banquet during which professional dancing is being performed for the entertainment of the guests. Though it is secular dancing that we have here the inscription is important from the present point of view, because the dancing, which is so graphically depicted, does not differ greatly from that shown on other Egyptian inscriptions, where it is unmistakably sacred. Egyptian inscriptions are those which offer most material here; one or two Hittite and Assyrian inscriptions are also available, and will be described later; but otherwise there is but little to be obtained from this source.

(2) Very prolific, on the other hand, is the second source, in the main, Greek. There are large numbers of vessels of different kinds—vases, bowls, cups, dishes, flasks, jugs, bottles, jars, pitchers, etc., on which dancing is depicted[2]; many of these represent secular dancing; some give dances of a quasi-religious kind, e.g. the dances of satyrs; but most of them depict religious dances, sometimes of gods and goddesses, at others of

[1] Numbered 37984.
[2] In the British Museum, e.g. see the specimens numbered B 36, B 167, B 625, B 643, E 20, E 35, E 137.

worshippers dancing in their honour; a very favourite subject is the dancing of Maenads. Belonging to this source are a variety of other kinds of vessels on which sacred dancing is depicted; sometimes the vessel itself is in the form of a sacred dance. Excavations in Cyprus have yielded some interesting material to which more detailed reference will be made below. Some coins have also been found which throw light on the subject. This source is, above all, valuable for showing us the kind of dances in vogue among the ancient Greeks, and bears out the truth of the remark that "the Greek dances may be divided and subdivided *ad infinitum*[1]."

(3) Our third source also offers abundance of material, viz. ancient literature; this source includes Egyptian literature (the Book of the Dead); the Old Testament and post-biblical Jewish literature; ancient Arabic literature; some of the ancient Church writers; and, above all, Greek and Latin classical authors, quotations from whom would alone fill a small volume.

(4) Lastly, there is modern literature. This must be divided into two classes. The first is a small and very unsatisfactory class: treatises which deal specifically with dancing. We have found this class of literature unsatisfactory for two reasons; first, because there is, comparatively, so little information of a tangible character to be gained from it; and, secondly, because no references are given to authorities, even when cited. Nevertheless, it is only fair to the respective authors to say that they are mainly concerned with modern dancing. As Crawley says, "there are no treatises written on any scientifically comprehensive lines[2]." With one exception,

[1] Lilly Grove, *op. cit.* p. 41.
[2] *ERE*, x. 362 *b*.

moreover, we have found the articles on the subject in all the well-known English and German Bible Dictionaries of extraordinarily little help. The exception is Hastings' *ERE*; here articles by Crawley, Farnell and Blackman have been of real help, and the writer gratefully acknowledges his indebtedness to them.

As to the other class of modern literature, it can only be described as limitless; we refer to the vast number of volumes dealing with uncultured races. To mention even a tithe of those which have been used would be out of the question; references to a good many will be found in the following pages. But it is impossible for the present writer not to say how much he owes to the works of Sir J. G. Frazer; without their stimulus these pages would never have been written.

The material contained in this source would fill a number of volumes; we have restricted ourselves to a certain number of more or less typical illustrations chosen from a great mass.

*　　*　　*　　*

More than a hundred and fifty years ago de Cahusac wrote in the Preface to his *Historical Treatise on Dancing*: "J'ai traité assez sérieusement un sujet qu'on ne regardera peut-être que comme très-futile." The present writer hopes and believes that his effort will not be regarded as "très-futile"; for we in these days have come to realize more fully than was possible in the eighteenth century the significance of the well-known words of Terence:

Homo sum; humani nihil a me alienum puto.

CHAPTER II

THE ORIGIN AND PURPOSES OF THE SACRED DANCE

I

I~N~ his thoughtful and very suggestive volume, *The Threshold of Religion*, Marett makes the assumption that an inductive study of the ideas and customs of savagery will show, firstly, that an awareness of a fundamental aspect of life and of the world, which aspect I shall provisionally term "supernatural," is so general as to be typical, and, secondly, that such an awareness is no less generally bound up with a specific group of vital reactions (p. 124).

Every student of such ideas and customs must know how thoroughly justified this assumption is. In studying the particular custom, and the ideas connected with it, with which we are here concerned, we find that this "awareness of the supernatural," together with the "vital reactions," are, at any rate in the earlier stages of its history, invariably present. That much, at all events, we have to go upon in seeking a theory as to the origin of the sacred dance. To account for its origin is, however, difficult; that is fully realized; and the present writer would desire to lay stress on the fact that as in seeking such origin he is largely in the domain of speculation and theory, nothing is further from his mind than to be dogmatic. The whole subject of the sacred dance has been so little dealt with excepting as a mere rite, that one is to a great extent on new ground; one must, therefore, be quite prepared to be convicted of fallacies.

That the sacred dance originated in pre-historic times goes without saying; but this means that no *proofs* can be adduced in support of any theory as to its origin; it must be a question of probabilities; perhaps only of possibilities. What is, however, certain is that since the sacred dance originated at a time when man was in a very primitive stage of culture, what first induced him to perform it must have been something very *naïve* and childlike. That, presumably, everyone would agree with. Now, there is no sort of doubt that one of the most ingrained characteristics of human nature is the imitative propensity. This is more pronounced in the child than in the grown man; and what holds good of the individual applies also to the race; the more uncultured man is, the more does he, mentally, approximate to the child; so that the further back we go in the history of the race, the more pronounced and childlike will be that imitative propensity. As Crawley has reminded us[1], Aristotle maintained that dancing is imitative; and in all its forms it is an artistic imitation of physical movement expressive of emotions or ideas. Rightly or wrongly, then, we believe that the sacred dance owes its origin to this imitative propensity in man.

Now, in the animistic stage what first suggested the presence of life in anything was movement. The cause of the movement was neither understood nor enquired into. A tree, swayed by the wind, moved; therefore it was alive. But it would not strike a more or less primitive savage that it was the wind which caused the movement. What he would instinctively have recognized was that here was something which he did not understand; and

---

[1] In *ERE*, x. 358 *a*; cp. Harrison, *op. cit.* p. 44; Leuba, *A Psychological Study of Religion*, pp. 62 f. (1912).

therefore there was a mystery about it which inspired awe. So, too, with streams, and rivers, and the sea; they were alive because they had motion. In course of time this would be modified in so far that the belief arose that the tree or stream contained life because of an indwelling spirit which caused the movement, thus indicating its presence; but even so, it would have been difficult for the savage to draw a distinction between the two at first. Whether the same course of savage "reasoning" will apply in regard to the sun, moon, and, later, to the stars, in the earlier stages of the period when he first began to take "reasoning" note of his surroundings, is doubtful; for it is probable that he looked around and downwards before he looked upwards. At any rate, sooner or later he would have realized that they too moved, and that therefore they were alive, either themselves, or animated by something, more probably by somebody. Thus motion, movement, which, on the analogy of man himself, was believed to denote life, was the first thing which the savage mind connected with supernatural powers[1].

We suggest, then, that the origin of the sacred dance was the desire of early man to imitate what he conceived to be the characteristic of supernatural powers. Not that this was, in the first instance, a dance in the generally accepted sense of the word; but merely a movement, whether in the form of the swaying of the body in imitation of trees, or a single-file running in imitation of a stream, or a more boisterous movement in imitation of the waves of the sea or of a storm-swept lake. The innate tendency to rhythmic motion would soon have asserted itself, and primitive dance, in the more usual sense,

[1] Prof. J. Y. Simpson, *Man and the Attainment of Immortality*, p. 115 (1922).

would result. But it would be a *sacred* dance in so far that it was performed in imitation of some supernatural power, vague and originally impersonal, as it undoubtedly was; to honour such by an imitative dance denotes a religious intention.

The reasonable objection will be urged that it was not only things which "moved" that early man regarded as living or as indwelt by a spirit, but that stones, for example, were among the very early things which were treated with veneration because they were believed to be the abodes of spirits; these did not move, so that the suggested theory of the origin of the sacred dance breaks down here. But when one seeks to penetrate the mind of uncultured man and to get behind his mental outlook, and especially when one contemplates the working of the child-mind which offers so many analogies with, and illustrations of that of the mentally immature savage, one becomes convinced that this veneration of stones, early as it was in the history of religion, was later than that of things which move. And the reason of this is simple; a moving thing attracts attention before that which does not move; that lies in the nature of things alike with the child and the savage mind. When once the moving things are believed to be the abodes of spirits, and the existence of these is universally recognized, then the further step that they exist in other things follows easily and naturally. We are thinking of the time when as yet early man was only impressed by those things which, because of their motion, attracted his attention.

Réville says that

the dance was the first and chief means adopted by prehistoric humanity of entering into active union with

the deity adored. The first idea was to imitate the
measured movements of the god, or at any rate what
were supposed to be such. Afterwards this fundamental
motive was forgotten, like so many other religious forms
which tradition and habit sustained even when the
spirit was gone[1].

We entirely agree; but the question is whether this does
not represent a later stage in the religion of prehistoric
humanity. Must there not have been a prior stage in
which a less concrete idea of supernatural powers obtained? What induced the supposition that the god
performed "measured movements"? And what would
have been thought to be the form of these movements?
Mr Marett, in the first essay of the volume already referred to, brings forward incontrovertible arguments, as
it seems to us, for believing that there was a stage in the
mental and religious development of man in which he
was not yet capable of other than a vague sense of the
supernatural; in which he had not yet associated definite
spirits or ghosts with what he conceived to be supernatural phenomena; but in which the sense of mystery
and consequently of awe in face of these supernatural
phenomena filled his heart. This is also dealt with in
the fourth essay: "The Conception of Mana." It is in
this stage that we would locate the origin of the sacred
dance, performed in imitation of what were the movements of supernatural powers, but powers of the vaguest
kind; merely a something, unknown, mysterious, and
therefore to be feared; but associate yourself with it,
and already you are in an indefinable way in communion
with it; you have in some sense made friends with it,

[1] *Lectures on the origin and growth of Religion, as illustrated by
the native religions of Mexico and Peru*, p. 224 (1895).

THE ORIGIN AND PURPOSES

18   THE ORIGIN AND PURPOSES

which makes things safer. "Given the supernatural in any form there are always two things to note about it: firstly, that you are to be heedful in regard to it; secondly, that it has power[1]." So that what Réville says is true, but it must be referred to a later stage of religious development.

Another consideration in connexion with the origin of the sacred dance must be briefly dealt with. Many savage peoples trace the origin of their sacred dances to various animals by which, as they maintain, they were taught to dance; therefore they imitate, in their dances, the movements of these animals. Thus, for example, we have kangaroo-dances, dog-dances, and cassowary-dances among the Monumbo of New Guinea[2]; bear-dances among the Carrier Indians[3], the Gilyaks (in Eastern Siberia), the women of Kamtchatka[4], and others. It may, therefore, be urged that the sacred dance originated in this way. But apart from other arguments, it will suffice to point out that to early man the sight of animals was probably so much in the natural order of things that there was nothing about them to strike him; in any case there was nothing supernatural or mysterious about them, nothing to be afraid about in the sense of fear inspired by the unknown. Such being the case there would have been no reason to imitate their movements, as there was in the case of what were to early man those mysterious powers whose movements he could not explain. The connexion of animals with gods, and the belief in descent from animals belong to subsequent

---

[1] Marett, *op. cit.* p. 127.
[2] Vormann, "Tänze und Tanzfestlichkeiten der Monumbo-Papua," in *Anthropos*, VI. 415 ff. (1911).
[3] Frazer, *GB, Balder the Beautiful*, II. 274 (1913).
[4] *GB, The Spirits of the Corn and of the Wild*, II. 190 f., 195 (1912).

ages; such conceptions necessitate reflexion during long periods of time. Therefore it cannot have been in imitation of animals that the sacred dance took its origin.

The theory as to the origin of the sacred dance suggested may or may not commend itself; but that it took its rise from supernatural powers of some sort seems certain; and this is supported by the belief of many savage peoples that their sacred dances were originally taught them by their gods[1]. The ancient Greeks also held that their sacred dances were performed in imitation of gods and goddesses. The Pyrrhic dance was said to have been the invention of the Dioscuri by some; others attributed it to Athena. Again, Artemis, Dionysos, and Zeus himself, were all believed to have set men the example of dancing. Hathor among the Egyptians and Baal-Marqôd among the Phoenicians are other examples. Is it not quite conceivable that this echoes what obtained in more primitive times?

II

We come now to consider the purposes of the sacred dance.

The whole idea and object of dancing, among civilized peoples, has now become so purely a matter of pastime and enjoyment that it is, at first, difficult to realize its very serious aspect among men in past ages, and among uncivilized races to-day. It may be true enough that dancing has always been a means of exercise and pleasure[2]; but from the earliest historical times—and, judging from what can be gathered from its very widespread practice among all known races of uncivilized men, the same is probably true of remote prehistoric times—this purpose

[1] See, e.g., Toy, op. cit. p. 491.
[2] Stow, The Native Races of South Africa, pp. 111 f.

has always been subordinated to religious uses primarily. There are, it is true, many instances among savages at the present day of dances being nothing more than a means of exercise and enjoyment; but it is not too much to assert that in every case the elimination of the religious element is due to extraneous influences. This is vividly illustrated in Polynesia, for example.

"Polynesian dancing," writes Mr Macmillan Brown, "has advanced far on the road to conventionalism. It has shed much of its pantomimic purpose and its religious meaning, and in this it reveals the collision of two or more cultures. In a region marked by so much that is so highly primitive, nothing but the clash of different religious systems could explain its divorce from rites and ceremonies and its appearance as an almost purely secular art, intended to amuse and delight an assembly of spectators."

The same writer shows that the character of the dancing among them presents the proof of its originally purely religious purpose; for

it is not like European dancing, a harmony of "twinkling feet." It is wholly occupied in posturing, waving the arms and bending the body, as if before a shrine. It is the upper part of the body that is chiefly engaged. Where the feet come in, it is only to effect the occasional advances or retreats, as if to or from the altar, or in the resounding thud of the war-dance. The Polynesian dance is oftenest stationary[1].

At the same time it would be a mistake to suppose that all religious dancing was necessarily of this more or less stationary character; we shall refer to examples of a very different kind below; but it is well to emphasize

---

[1] *Maori and Polynesian, their origin, history, and culture,* p. 203 (1907).

the truth that all dancing was originally religious, and was performed for religious purposes.

Of course it often happens that the different objects of the dance coalesce; religious and secular, or religious and utilitarian, or more than one religious purpose, being combined in the same dance; this, as we shall see, is illustrated in Israelite practice. Nevertheless, it is very certain that in numberless instances all feelings of enjoyment had ceased though the dance continued hour after hour because it was believed that a sacred duty was being performed thereby. The young North American Dakotahs, for example, did not go on dancing for a couple of days because they were so enamoured of it; nor was it for pastime that the Thyiads danced on madly in honour of Dionysos until they dropped to the ground unconscious. The reasons which made this sort of thing necessary are absurd to us, but from the point of view of antique thought it was a very serious and solemn matter.

It is this serious aspect of our subject upon which stress must be laid because now-a-days we naturally think of dancing as mere enjoyment and pastime. Some of the dances and their objects, and the ways in which they are performed, among savages are so funny that they would, we imagine, provoke a smile on the face of a sphinx, were it capable of doing such a thing; but while, at times, we cannot resist a laugh, we shall do well to remember that it was far from being a laughing matter to the savage; to do him justice we must seek to get to the back of his mind, to enter into his feelings, and to look at things through his eyes; then it will be realized what the sacred dance meant to him, and its essential seriousness will become apparent.

What the sacred dance meant not only to uncivilized men, but also to the most cultured races of antiquity, will be seen from the purposes for which it was performed. These we will now briefly enumerate.

(*a*) It was, first and foremost, performed for the purpose of honouring what were regarded as supernatural powers[1]. In the pre-animistic stage these powers were entirely vague and undefined; in the animistic stage they developed into spirits, some benevolent, others maleficent, powerful for good or evil. Later they became gods and goddesses. *Why* dancing was a means of honouring these supernatural, later superhuman, powers was for these reasons: It was supposed to be an act of imitation, and therefore flattering to the higher power (the imitative propensity in man has already been referred to). Secondly, by "taking it out of yourself" in the presence of the power or deity you were offering something in the nature of a propitiation, whether as a gift or as an act of self-sacrifice; in either case it would be honouring the higher power. This taking it out of oneself in honour of a spirit or a god is an interesting phenomenon, and in one form or another has asserted itself throughout the history of religion. It is the earliest form of what in course of time showed itself in such things as self-castigation and self-mortification; its extreme form being the love of martyrdom; for to whatever degree the cult of self may have entered into these things, it would be grossly unfair not to recognize that they were believed to be pleasing in the sight of the deity, and that they were, therefore, done with a view to honouring him.

(*b*) Psychologically connected with the foregoing we have as another purpose of the sacred dance that of

[1] Cp. de Cahusac, *op. cit.* p. 38.

"showing-off" before a higher power. One must enter into the child-mind in order to grasp what a real thing this is. The close analogy between the way-of-thinking in the child and in the more or less primitive savage has already been referred to, and is recognized on all hands. Here are two cases of great interest which vividly illustrate the point under consideration. The present writer vouches for the literal truth of each. A little girl, not exceeding five years, was dancing before a picture of the Madonna and Child; after her dance she turned to her mother and said: "Do you think the Baby Jesus liked to see me dance?" It is not quite easy to say in this case in how far the purpose was to please the "Baby Jesus," and in how far the perfectly natural and innocent purpose was to "show off" before Him; probably both motives were combined. But the second is purely one of "showing off." A child of about three, a boy this time, kept on jumping as high as he could in the fields; presently his father heard him say: "See, God, how high I can jump!" We could hardly have more delightful and instructive illustrations of the innate desire, common to the child and to man of immature mental development, to show what they can do in the sight of their betters. So that we may justly reckon among the purposes of the sacred dance this desire to "show off" before a superhuman power, or what is conceived to be such.

(c) Next; the honour done to the higher power by means of imitation had, in the eyes of uncivilized man, some important consequences which offer further reasons why the sacred dance was performed. Just as in imitative magic the thing imitated was thereby effected, so by imitating the supernatural power the imitator conceived himself to be making himself one with him who was imitated. This purpose of the sacred dance would not, however, have belonged to the earliest stage, for it presupposes the recognition of personality in the supernatural power, and that points to a distinct advance; and the possibility is worth contemplating as to whether, and in how far, the sacred dance may have contributed to this advance. At any rate, this idea that an undefined union was brought about by means of the sacred dance seems to be the precursor of the more developed form of the same idea that union could be brought about by personating a god or a goddess. When, for example, men and women, by disguising themselves as horses, cats, pigs, or hares, personated Demeter and Persephone, and danced in their honour, they believed that they were, in some inexplicable way, united with these goddesses. In the earlier stage, by imitating what a god *does*, *i.e.* dancing, union with him is effected; in the later stage, the like result is achieved by imitating what he *is*, and dancing in that guise. At the bottom of all this lies the principle which looms so large in savage philosophy that "like produces like," *i.e.* sympathetic magic which assumes that

things act on each other at a distance through a secret sympathy, the impulse being transmitted from one to the other by means of what we may conceive as a kind of invisible ether, not unlike that which is postulated by modern science for a precisely similar purpose, namely, to explain how things can physically affect each other through a space which appears to be empty[1].

As is well known, a more pronounced and realistic means of union was that of eating the flesh or drinking

[1] Frazer, *GB*, *The Magic Art and the Evolution of Kings*, I. 54 (1911).

the blood of a sacrificial victim which represented the god; by receiving the god into himself a man became identified with the god. So that we have in the course of the development of religious thought and practice, in a materialistically ascending scale, three means whereby union with a supernatural power was believed to be effected: imitation, personation, and the act which produced identification. But the important point for our present purpose, and it is one which needs emphasis, is that over and over again it is found that the two latter rites (*i.e.* those of personation and of absorbing the god) are accompanied by the sacred dance as a necessary adjunct. It may be argued that this is merely done on the principle of making certainty doubly certain; but it is at least possible that we have here a case of the retention of the earliest rite simply because it *is* the earliest. We are bound to look for great *naïveté* in considering the ideas and practices of backward races—and, indeed, not only backward races where religious rites are concerned; —and if, in course of time, new means suggested themselves of uniting oneself with a god or goddess, it is quite in accordance with what we know of uncivilized man to suppose that he continued the older method side by side with the newer ones, even though there was not much meaning attached to it.

This theory that one of the earliest purposes of the sacred dance was to imitate what supernatural powers did, and that this imitation was believed to be the means of union with this supernatural being (as it came to be), receives some support and confirmation from what we know to have been the purpose of the ecstatic dance.

(*d*) Uncultured man believed that by dancing to such an extent that he became unconscious he was not only doing something that was honouring to the deity, not only offering something in the nature of sacrifice, but that he was, above all, making his body a fit temporary abode for his god. He did not enquire how this came about. Conceivably, the earliest idea, though unexpressed, was that by honouring the god to this extent the god showed his approval by uniting himself with his dancing worshipper. The earlier widespread belief that the deity took up his abode at certain times in trees, stones, etc., may well have suggested the possibility of the same thing occurring in men, but more especially in those more intimately and directly dedicated to his worship. The question would have arisen as to the means to be employed whereby this end could be achieved in the case of men; and as dancing was the earliest form of worship this would have been the most natural means to suggest itself. The dance would then proceed; during it the performers would be anxiously awaiting some inner indication of the entrance of the deity; nothing, of course, would happen until the long-continued dance would induce first giddiness, then semi-consciousness, and finally a state of semi-delirium ending not infrequently in total unconsciousness for some time. But it is easy to understand that the first signs of semi-consciousness would have been interpreted as the advent of the deity and the beginnings of the divine overpowering. Given belief in the possibility of divine indwelling in a man, the further belief that the god utilized his worshipper as his mouthpiece was a natural and easy transition. Natural, because it could not be supposed that the god would take up his abode in a man without some purpose, and what more obvious purpose than that of making his will known? Easy, because the

mechanism, if one may so call it, of utterance was all
ready to hand.   Other things would follow, also in the
natural course; for if, on the one hand, the god utilized
the body of his worshipper as the vehicle for making his
will known, the worshipper could, on the other hand,
utilize the divine power with which he was suffused for
other purposes. Thus, for example, we have the Hebrew
prophet who, in an ecstatic state, utters the will of
Jahwe, or gives an oracle; or, as illustrating the other
side, we have the Bodo-priest "devil-dancer" of
Southern India who utilizes the divine power within
him for working cures.

But whatever the result might be, the important thing
from our present point of view is that the requisite state
required for the accomplishment of these things was
brought about by the performance of the sacred dance.

The ecstatic dance will receive a good deal of notice
below (pp. 107 ff.), so that we need not say more about
it here.

(e) Another purpose of the sacred dance was to make
the crops grow, or of helping, or inducing the god to do
so. From one point of view here the sacred dance was
an act of imitative magic. Thus, by a dance in which
the chief characteristic was high leaps it was believed
by many peoples that the corn would grow high. It is
probable, as Frazer suggests, that this was at any rate
one of the purposes with which the Salii, the priests of
the old Italian god of vegetation, danced high and leapt.
As an act of imitative magic, again, the sacred dance
had among some peoples the purpose of helping the sun
to run his course. For example, this was probably at
one time of its history the object of "Ariadne's Dance";
and the dance known by the name of the "Labyrinth"

may well have been believed to assist the stars in their courses. These, and many other examples, are dealt with in the following pages.

(*f*) Further, there are instances on record of the sacred dance having the purpose of hallowing or consecrating a victim for sacrifice, as in the case of the Arabs performing a processional dance round a camel destined for sacrifice, or of the Israelites making the circuit round the altar, or of the Kayans of Sarāwak circling round their sacrificial pigs. In all such cases it is an act of consecration by means of the magic circle.

(*g*) As an adjunct to initiation ceremonies the sacred dance was also believed to serve some useful purpose. Presumably it was an act of homage to the god or goddess who was supposed to be present. This is suggested by the dancing at the Brauronian ceremonies of Artemis which, according to Farnell, was a kind of initiation ceremony by which young girls were consecrated to the service of this goddess.

(*h*) There are some grounds for the belief that the sacred dance was sometimes performed with the purpose of assisting warriors to gain a victory in battle; here, too, it was an act of imitative magic. It had, in this connexion, the further purpose of appeasing the spirits of slain enemies.

(*i*) As a marriage rite the sacred dance, at any rate during some time of its history, fulfilled, as was believed, one or two important purposes. The reference to the "Sword-dance" in the Old Testament is in all probability a relic of the antique custom of combating the vague dangers which were supposed to menace those entering upon the marriage state. These dangers, undefined but nevertheless very real to those who believed in their existence, arose not only from the fact of the new conditions of life that were beginning, but also because of a reciprocal fear on the part of the sexes, and a close contact between them emphasized this. Another way of combating, or at least averting these dangers, was by means of a change of identity; hence the once world-wide custom, still in existence in some countries, of the bridal couple assuming "royal" state, and being treated as king and queen during the period of the wedding festivities.

Further, there are some reasons for thinking that the sacred dance as a marriage rite sometimes had the purpose of bringing about a fruitful marriage; there are certain ceremonies during the period of celebration in which the dance figures prominently which point to this, and the analogy of the dance for making the crops grow offers some corroboration.

(j) There are special purposes for which the sacred dance was performed as a mourning or a burial rite. At times these are of a curiously contradictory character. The ghosts of the dead number among them those who are kindly disposed towards the living, and those who are malevolent in their attitude towards them; the latter are supposed to be able to do harm. Speaking quite generally, it appears, upon the whole, that the less advanced the cultural stage the greater the tendency to regard the spirits of the departed as malevolent. Since the various races from which illustrations of the sacred dance as a mourning rite are gathered were, or are (as the case may be), in different stages of civilization, it follows that the purposes of the rite vary; for the belief regarding the attitude of the dead towards the living has a good deal to do with the purpose for which the

sacred dance was performed. Thus we find that it sometimes has the object of driving away the ghost of the departed; or else there will be a dance on the grave for the
purpose of preventing the ghost from roaming. At other
times it is the means of scaring away evil spirits who are
believed to congregate in the vicinity of a corpse. Very
strange, but interesting, is the custom among some races
of personating the dead in the sacred dance; this is supposed to be a potent means of bringing him back, and
he is believed to join the survivors in the dance; he is
present, but invisible, in the man who personates him.
This reminds one of the union with a supernatural spirit
by imitating him in the dance, to which reference has
been made above; the same idea underlies each. But
the purpose of the sacred dance as a mourning or burial
rite which appears as the most usual is that of honouring
the departed. This is doubtless very frequently simply
a mark of affection; but at other times it is in the nature
of a propitiatory act whereby the spirit of the departed
is persuaded to refrain from molesting the living.

Many illustrations of these various purposes of the
sacred dance will be offered in the following pages.

CHAPTER III

THE SACRED DANCE AMONG
THE ISRAELITES

I

So far as the Old Testament is concerned this subject of the dance in religious ritual illustrates a fact which biblical study, on the comparative basis, is bringing more and more into prominence, and which needs to be recognized both in the interests of truth and in order to realize more fully the evolutionary development of religion as an eternal principle in the divine economy. The original aims and objects of the sacred dance were, as we have seen, "primitive"; the continuance of the rite throughout the ages, even to comparatively recent times among practically all peoples, does not in any way detract from the truth of this, for everyone knows with what persistency religious custom and ritual continues, not only after the original object and meaning has been forgotten, but even when it has no meaning at all. Its existence among the Israelites, therefore, shows them to have been and to have acted throughout their religious history as other races did in this respect (and it is only one of many other illustrations that could be given), in spite of what we rightly believe to have been special opportunities for more exalted forms of worship.

It must be confessed that the religious uniqueness of the Israelites, as a nation, has been, and often still is, exaggerated to an undue extent. Certainly there were among them those who may well be described as unique, *sui generis*; but they were the great exceptions. The nation as a whole was for many centuries no better and no worse than others; and what stronger evidence for this could be afforded than that given in the prophetical books of the Old Testament? Its ultimate emergence from the religious norm of the world to a position of isolated superiority was due to a mere handful of men who offered the greatest example that the world had hitherto seen of what could be accomplished by subordinating will and personality to the influence and guidance of the Divine Creator.

True, it was among some of these very prophets that the most interesting kind of sacred dance—the ecstatic dance —was in vogue, with its wildness and extravagances; in this they, or at least the earliest of them, did not differ from certain classes of "holy men" all the world over; where they did differ was in their development of the conception which underlay the purpose of the ecstatic dance, *i.e.* union with the deity; and it is just here that they stand out in such bold relief from all others. The earliest prophets believed that this sacred dance was the means whereby the divine spirit came upon them; this belief they shared with others; but they rose to the higher belief that *this* means was not necessary for achieving the purpose for which it was used. It had served a useful purpose; but having served its purpose it was dropped. The prophets came to the realization that there were more spiritual means whereby union with the deity was brought about; then the sacred dance found no further place among them. They shed the husk, but retained the kernel. It was the same principle upon which St Paul acted in later days in regard to the Law. The sacred dance, too, was in its way a "school-

master" (Gal. iii. 24), leading men to better things.
When, centuries later, the far more cultured Greeks were
still "raving" in honour of Dionysos, the Hebrew prophets had long since learned that it is God Himself Who
puts His spirit upon men (cp. Isa. xlii. 1), and that this
is not a thing to be effected by the will or act of man.
"Who hath directed the Spirit of Jahwe?" asks one of
them in fine irony (Isa. xl. 13).

Thus the history of the ecstatic dance among the
Hebrew prophets is one of many illustrations showing
their uniqueness.

It is not, however, with these extraordinarily gifted
prophets that we are now concerned. We are thinking
of the very ordinary and very human Israelites as a
whole who, like innumerable men and women of other
races, were endowed with emotions and aspirations which
were common to humanity. And it is a curious but
interesting phenomenon that the sacred dance was among
the Israelites, as among all other peoples, one of the means
whereby these emotions and aspirations were expressed.

The fact that in the Mosaic legislation no provision is
made for ritual dancing when so many other minute
details of ritual are given might seem to suggest that
such a thing was discountenanced. Without question it
is true to say that "the priestly historians and legislators resolutely excluded, as far as possible, everything
that could infer any similarity between the worship of
Jahwe and that of heathen deities[1]." But it is doubtful
whether the subject of the sacred dance would have
come into consideration in such a connexion; it was a
practice too deeply ingrained in human nature as a
means of expressing religious emotion to suggest that it

[1] Millar in Hastings' *DB*, i. 550 *b*.

implied assimilation to heathen worship. The bringing
of oblations, the offering of sacrifices, were also common
to Israelite and heathen worship, but that similarity
would never have struck the Israelite legislators as de-
rogatory, because these, too, were means of expressing
religious emotion which, in one form or another, were
common to all races. The Mosaic legislation makes no
provision for the posture to be assumed in the presence
of the deity, nor does it say anything about singing in
worship; but it is difficult to believe that there were not
fixed modes in regard to these which had been in vogue
from time immemorial; and therefore they needed no
mention. The same may be postulated in the case of the
sacred dance. A thing which all the evidence shows to
have been a world-wide means of expressing religious
emotion and of honouring the deity during a long period
in the history of religious development, was not likely
to have been wanting among the Israelites.

In those passages in the Old Testament in which religious dancing is recorded there is no hint of disapproval,
let alone prohibition. It is, therefore, evident that it
must have been looked upon as a usual and integral
part of worship. It must also be remembered that the
sacred dance continued to be an important element in
worship on special occasions among the Jews in post-
biblical times; the evidence will be considered later. That
this could have been an innovation is out of the question;
it was merely the continuation, in some cases quite
possibly an elaboration, of a rite familiar to the people
from time immemorial.

The comparatively rare mention, therefore, of the
sacred dance in the Old Testament must not mislead us;
the reasons for that are very natural. And when it is

realized what a number of words there are in Hebrew for dancing (see pp. 44 ff.), and that only once is there a possible reference to secular, as distinct from religious, dancing, the conclusion will be forced upon us that it played a much larger *rôle* in the religious life of the people than first appearances would seem to indicate.

As far as can be gathered, religious dancing among the Israelites was, as a general rule, performed by the sexes separately; in the account of the worship of the Golden Calf, however, it must be allowed that the possibility of promiscuous dancing is not excluded, see especially Exod. xxxii. 2, 3. Among other peoples it is found that, mostly, the sacred dance was performed by men and women separately; but there are notable exceptions among the Egyptians as well as the Syrians, also among the Greeks; and the same applies to the uncultured races.

II

When all the *data* in the Old Testament have been gathered it is possible to discern certain types of the sacred dance; by this we do not necessarily mean varieties of mode, not but that these also occur; the type is indicated rather by the connexion in which the dance occurs. Therefore, although it is not to be supposed that there was, generally speaking, any idea of having particular kinds of dance reserved for different occasions, it is possible to attempt some kind of classification. At any rate, it is a convenient method to adopt in reviewing the evidence.

Emphasis must again be laid on the fact that when one is speaking of the "sacred dance" in past ages one has to allow to the term a wide connotation. We have come to use the word "dance" in a very restricted sense;

in antiquity it was different; included in it are modes varying from a staid, march-like rhythmic step, to the wilder movements of the ecstatic dance. (1) We draw attention first to the sacred *processional dance.* A cursory reference to one or two examples will suffice here as a more detailed examination of each type of dance will be found in the chapters to follow. Judging from the few *data* offered by the Old Testament, the sacred processional dance among the Israelites was always performed in honour of Jahwe. In the well-known instance of David and the Israelites dancing in procession before the Ark, it is really in the presence of Jahwe that it takes place since He is conceived as being present in the Ark. The dance assumes various forms according to the degree of religious excitement engendered. It is spoken of as being dancing of the ordinary kind, *i.e.* the common Hebrew word for dancing is used; but presently it takes on the character of a rotating dance, then there is jumping followed by something in the nature of skipping, and it is also spoken of as a whirling movement. It will be noticed that five different words are used here to express the different ways in which the dancing was performed. Although the occasion on which this took place was a very special one, it would be a mistake to suppose that the sacred dance was only reserved for such special occasions. It is rather to be gathered from the incidental way in which the dancing is mentioned that the rite was usual, and was only of a more elaborate character because of the special occasion. A single mention of this kind must, it may be safely asserted, imply a well-known and usual custom, otherwise it would be commented upon as something out of the ordinary.

(2) The sacred dance also takes the form of *encircling a sacred object,* either an idol, or a sacrificial victim, or an altar; in this last case the sacrificial victim would, of course, be included. The form of this type of dance was either a march-like step or a running step or else the worshippers held hands and danced round. This latter is nowhere specifically mentioned in the Old Testament; but it is such an obvious form for a dance to take that we can scarcely doubt its having existed among the Israelites. Besides, interesting examples of a concrete kind have been found depicting this form of dance round sacred objects which quite possibly owe their origin to Semitic inspiration; some of these are described in Chapter VI below. This encircling dance was undoubtedly an act of worship; it is also possible that in some cases it was intended to have a consecrating effect either upon the worshippers or upon the sacrificial victim; in the example given by Nilus (see p. 95) the latter would seem to have been the case. The theory of some scholars that the circle dance was a symbolic representation of the movement of the heavenly bodies has also a good deal to commend it. As a funeral rite this form of the sacred dance served some other purposes (see below).

(3) The *ecstatic dance* is that which has received most attention from scholars, and deservedly, for it is one of the most curious phenomena in the history of religious ritual. In the exuberance of emotion engendered by it the performers experienced what appeared to them to amount, for the time being, almost to a metamorphosis; they believed themselves to be infused and permeated by the influence—perhaps it would be truer to say the essence—of the deity in whose honour they were dancing. Thus came about what was conceived to be in some

mystic, but wholly inexplicable way, a union with the deity adored. In the Old Testament we have the well-known example of the prophets performing this dance in 1 Sam. x. 5 ff.; its contagious character is graphically illustrated by the case of Saul, whose condition becomes such that the people ask: "Is Saul also among the prophets?" and he is spoken of as having been "turned into another man" because as a result of the ecstatic dance the spirit of Jahwe came mightily upon him. The language implies that when once the required condition has been reached it is then Jahwe Who takes the initiative; the body as such remains a passive instrument, but it becomes a Beth-el, a temporary house of God from which He speaks forth through the medium of the voice of the possessed.

As in the case of other types of the sacred dance, there cannot be anything unique about this even though it is only referred to once or twice in the Old Testament; its incidental mention without further comment stamps it as being nothing out of the ordinary.

Another form of this ecstatic type of dance is mentioned in the Old Testament, also in connexion with prophets, though not Israelite prophets. There was a peculiar kind of limping dance performed, as it would appear, on special occasions by the prophets of Baal. This began with a limping step round the altar as though the performers were lame, but soon developed into a wild jumping about on the altar, and culminated in self-laceration with knives and the like. In how far a state of semi-consciousness or total unconsciousness was attained is not indicated; but in the light of analogous cases (referred to in Chapter VII) it may be gathered that the loss of the physical sensation of pain inflicted by the self-laceration must imply to some extent a loss of consciousness so far as external surroundings were concerned. In writing about the prophetic ecstasy of Syrian as well as Israelite prophets, Dr T. H. Robinson well expresses the state in saying that it was

a peculiar psychic condition in which the subject seemed to be possessed of powers, indeed of a whole sphere of consciousness, which was denied to the ordinary individual, and to the prophet himself in normal states. He did not cease to be conscious of the world as it appeared to others, but he heard and saw things which were beyond their range. There were a number of well-marked physical phenomena connected with the condition of ecstasy, though these were not invariable. The subject might be affected with a certain constriction of the muscles, in which case the state resembled that of a trance. On the other hand, muscular activity might be largely increased. Leaping, bodily contortions, and loud cries resulted, which, as they tended to become regular and rhythmical, developed into dancing and song. The subject frequently experienced a kind of anaesthesia, and would slash wildly at his own body with knife or whip, without showing any signs of physical pain[1].

We shall find all this illustrated in the examples, to be given in Chapter VII, of this type of dance among a number of races.

Various means were employed to bring about this ecstatic state, such as alcohol, and other drugs; but there can be little doubt that the most frequent, and certainly the most primitive, means adopted was that of dancing.

(4) The kind of sacred dance which was the most common among the Israelites, as among other peoples, was that proper to *Vintage and Harvest Festivals*. That

---

[1] *The Classical Quarterly*, October 1907, pp. 202 f.

it seems, from the scanty references to it which we have in the Old Testament, as well as from many indications in regard to its performance among other races, largely to have lost its sacred character will not deceive us as to its originally religious purpose. It was a characteristic of Israelite worship that the note of joy should sound during its celebration; the command: "Ye shall rejoice before Jahwe your God" sufficiently bears this out. Apart, therefore, from the original purpose of this kind of sacred dance to which reference will be made in Chapter VIII, there is no reason to doubt that Vintage and Harvest dances among the Israelites were essentially of a religious character, although the rejoicing, of which dancing was one of the most natural modes of expression, might not always appeal to some of the more austere prophets, see, *e.g.*, Amos v. 21–23. The very rare specific mention in the Old Testament of the festival dances is quite comprehensible, for what was obviously proper to the celebration of a feast it would be superfluous to speak about. Moreover, there is ample evidence in post-biblical Jewish literature of the existence of the sacred dance at festivals.

(5) *Dances in celebration of victory* in battle are referred to several times in the Old Testament. Taking the passages in which these are mentioned by themselves the custom of which they speak is nothing more than a simple and natural expression of joy and thanksgiving for victory. But all such customs have a long history behind them; and when analogous customs among other, less civilized, peoples are considered, some points of interest and significance emerge which suggest the possibility of the custom being, in its origin, due to a different and more practical cause. There are some grounds for

believing that the custom of which the Old Testament speaks was a remnant of what was originally a dance performed by women which had for its object the helping of the men to gain a victory by means of imitative magic. In the Old Testament there is, of course, no trace of this beyond the fact that the dance was performed by women; and it has become simply an act of joyful thanksgiving to God and a tribute to the returning victors. It is necessary to consider the analogous rite in its earlier forms as seen among peoples of lower civilization to estimate what justification there may be for this supposition. If it should be the fact that this type of dance was, in its origin, a means of effecting victory by magic, it would be an interesting illustration of magic being, as Marett says, "part and parcel of the 'god-stuff' out of which religion fashions itself[1]." Indeed, when dealt with in detail, this subject of the sacred dance in the Old Testament receives its chief interest and importance from the fact that at all events some of the types there mentioned are illustrations of the development of religion out of magic.

(6) There is some reason to believe that the sacred dance had a part to play during *the rite of circumcision*; late Rabbinic tradition seems to imply as much. It had its place among the Arabs on such occasions; and at initiation ceremonies all the world over the sacred dance was essential.

(7) Once more, the sacred dance during the *Wedding ceremony*, though only once implied in the Old Testament, was in all probability a regular institution; post-biblical Jewish literature offers presumptive evidence of its existence in earlier times among the Israelites.

---

[1] *Op. cit.* p. 66, the expression is Hartland's.

(8) And lastly, we have the sacred dance as a *Burial
rite*. As in other cases we have to rely, firstly, on the
evidence of later Jewish literature, and, secondly, upon
the analogous practice among other peoples. As we shall
show, the emotions of fear, honour, and love, which
according to the cultural stages of uncivilized men are
felt for the spirits of the departed, are such as are
common to mankind; and these emotions are expressed,
among other ways, by means of the sacred dance. What
cultural stage, or stages, are represented in the Old
Testament as that, or those, through which the Israelites
passed may well be a matter of difference of opinion; but
that in both thought and practice they were, as a whole,
in many respects no more advanced than other contemporary peoples does not admit of doubt. So that
when we find this rite in existence at burials or during
the mourning period among other Semites, and among
the Egyptians, not to mention the Greeks, the presumption is justified that the Israelites practised it too.

* * * *

In regard to much that has been said we are prepared
for the objection that the evidence of the Old Testament
does not offer sufficient justification for the assumptions
made. We agree that this is so if we are to rely upon
the Old Testament alone. But the object of the whole
of our investigation will be to show that the beliefs and
practices of any one race of people must, to do them full
justice, be studied in the light of analogous beliefs and
practices of other peoples. Only so can one fill up the
lacunae which inevitably exist in the records of the
races of antiquity. We have chosen as our illustration a
rite which may, likely enough, be regarded as of very

secondary importance; yet it is one which the evidence shows was at one time regarded as essential to man. It is therefore a study worth undertaking; for apart from its interest as a mere antiquarian investigation, we hope that it may be found to throw some modest side-lights on various other subjects.

CHAPTER IV

THE OLD TESTAMENT TERMS FOR "DANCING"

I

How large a *rôle* dancing in its various forms must have played among the Israelites is shown by the fact that, either in the restricted or in the more extended sense, no less than eleven Hebrew roots are used to describe its different characteristics. This in what is a relatively poor language is not without significance.

Before saying something about the meaning of these roots it will be well to give a list of them:

Sāḥaq and *tzāḥaq*, used in the intensive *piel* form.

Ḥūl.

Kārar, used in the *pilpel* form, also intensive.

Pāzaz, used in the *piel* form.

Rāqad, used in the *piel* form.

Sābab, used in the *hiphil*, causative, form.

Qāphatz, used in the *piel* form.

Dālag.

Tzāla', occurs only once.

Ḥāgag.

Pāsaḥ, used in the *piel* form.

The first thing to notice here is that most of these roots, when used in reference to dancing, occur only in intensive forms; this is significant as pointing to the nature and character of the sacred dance. Of the exceptions, *ḥūl* "to whirl" is intensive in its root-meaning; it has no *piel*, and its other forms occur only rarely, and almost entirely in the later poetical books. The roots *dālag* and *tzāla'* refer to a particular kind of ritual step; and as to *ḥāgag* more will be said in a moment.

Now as to the meaning of these different words for dancing:

The root *sāḥaq*, in its intensive form *siḥēq*, means in the first instance "to laugh," and it is also used in the sense of "playing" (Job xl. 29) and "merry-making" (Jer. xv. 17, xxx. 19, xxxi. 4, Zech. viii. 5; cp. also Judg. xvi. 25). In the specific sense of "dancing" it occurs in 1 Sam. xviii. 7: "...and the dancing women answered one another and said..." (see also 1 Chron. xv. 29). Equivalent to this root is *tzāḥaq*, also used in the intensive form *tziḥēq*, which occurs, *e.g.*, in Exod. xxxii. 6: "The people sat down to eat and drink, and rose up to dance." It is also used of "playing" or "sporting," *e.g.* Gen. xxi. 9, Judg. xvi. 25, but in the second of these passages its obvious meaning is "to dance," for as we shall see later this was the custom at feasts. This root, therefore, presents dancing in the aspect of a pleasant and enjoyable pastime. Further, in various passages this root is used as a parallel to other words for dancing. For example, in 1 Sam. xviii. 6, 7 just cited, it occurs as a parallel to the root which is the one most frequently used in the Old Testament for dancing, viz. *ḥūl*. This root expresses the "whirl" of the dance (*e.g.* Judg. xxi. 21, 23, Ps. lxxxvii. 7). It is the word used of the "writhing" or "twisting" of a woman in travail, *e.g.* Isa. xxvi. 17, xlv. 10, or of one in great pain, Isa. xiii. 8, xxiii. 5, Jer. li. 29; so that when used in the sense of dancing, contortions of the body are thought of, which suggests something of a rather wild character.

The "whirling" idea is also contained in the root *kārar* (in its intensive *pilpel* form, *kirkēr*), "to whirl about," or "rotate." It occurs, in this sense, only once in the

Old Testament, 2 Sam. vi. 14–16, of David dancing before Jahwe[1]; and in this passage we have another root which does not occur elsewhere in the sense of dancing, viz. *pāzaz* (again in the intensive form *pizzēz*); this expresses the idea of agile leaping as part of the dance[2], the cognate Arabic root means "to be excited." The idea of leaping is also contained in another root *rāqad* (in its intensive form *riqqēd*) which in its ordinary sense means "to skip about[3]"; as applied to dancing it occurs in the passage last mentioned, and see further, Isa. xiii. 21, Job xxi. 11, Joel ii. 5, Eccles. iii. 4, 1 Chron. xv. 29; in Ps. xxix. 6 it is used of a calf "skipping."

The root *sābab*, used of "going round" the altar, is spoken about below (pp. 93 f.), so that we can leave this for the present.

So far, then, we have briefly touched on words used in reference to dancing which either express or suggest the ideas of its being something enjoyable, of its involving the bending about of the body, whirling about, leaping, and skipping; as well as that of forming a circle, perhaps round the altar, but in any case encircling something, or going round about it.

Now we come to some rather special words. In including *dālag* in our category we realize that this is only justified because we are using the word "dancing" in its extended, as well as in its more restricted, sense; and we have shown above that this is not only permitted, but necessary in view of the general ideas underlying the whole subject. This word is used of the "leaping" of a

[1] In the Targum of Isa. lxvi. 20, however, we have the noun *kirkerān* (fem. plur.) meaning "dances."

[2] In Neo-Hebrew the word means "to dance."

[3] In the Midrash *Bemidbar Rabba* to xx. 11 it is said: "When a man plans a sin Satan dances before him...."

hart in Isa. xxxv. 6, just as the word *rāqad* is used, as
we have seen, of the "skipping" of a calf; the latter, as
already pointed out, occurs in several passages in the
sense of "dancing"; *dālag* may, therefore, be regarded
as in some sense parallel to it. In Cant. ii. 8 *dālag* certainly seems to refer to some form of dancing. But in
two other passages the word has a special sense; in these,
though the reference is not to dancing in the strict
meaning of the term, it is used of a ritual step of a
leaping character, and may justifiably be applied to
dancing in the more extended sense. Thus, in 1 Sam. v. 5
it is said that no one ever treads on the threshold of
Dagon's house in Ashdod. This is explained in the
Septuagint by the addition of the words "leaping over
they leap over"; this is probably only an explanatory
gloss (though it is conceivable that they represent a text
in which *dālōg yidlōgū* occurred), but it witnesses, at any
rate, to what was a well-known custom, for in the other
passage, Zeph. i. 9, punishment is pronounced against
"all those who leap over the threshold," without further
explanation, showing that something quite familiar is
being referred to. There was a similar Persian custom
which forbad stepping on the threshold, one had to leap
over it with the right foot first. The custom was due
to the belief that evil spirits crouched down on the
threshold, and the leaping over it prevented coming
into contact with them, and the consequent risk of
harm. The action implied the recognition of an alien
cult, hence its prohibition[1]. In Cant. ii. 8 the root

---

[1] The underlying idea regarding the threshold has continued
through the ages in many localities, witches having taken the
place frequently of evil spirits. Walpurgis Night (the eve of
May Day) is the special time for their activity, and leaping over
the threshold is then a necessary precaution.

qāphatz is used as a parallel to *dālag*, and also means "to jump," or the like; but this is the only passage in which the word is used in this sense. We come now to two roots of which rather more must be said. The first is *ḥāgag*. In 1 Sam. xxx. there is the account of David's attack on an Amalekite troop who had carried off all the women from Ziklag, among them his two wives; the Egyptian slave of an Amalekite, who had been abandoned by his master because he had fallen sick, is asked by David to lead him to the spot where the Amalekites were encamped; this he undertakes to do on condition that no harm comes to him; then we read in verse 16: "And when he had brought him down, behold, they were sprawling about all over the ground, eating and drinking and feasting" (*hōgĕgim*); that is how the Revised Version renders this last word. To render it thus, however, is pleonastic, for if they were eating and drinking they were quite obviously "feasting"; the word, therefore, cannot well have this meaning here. The more natural rendering would be "dancing"; and, indeed, this would be the meaning that we should expect, for, as will be shown below, "dancing" is almost synonymous with "feasting," because it was characteristic of feasts. Driver, in discussing this passage, says in reference to the word:

Whether, however, the sense of *dancing* is really expressed by the word is very doubtful. Modern lexicographers only defend it by means of the questionable assumption that *ḥāgag* may have had a similar signification to *ḥūg*, which, however, by no means itself expresses the sense of *to dance*, but *to make a circle* (Job xxvi. 10)....It is best to acquiesce in the cautious judgement of Nöldeke[1], who declares that he cannot

---

[1] *Zeitschrift der Deutschen Morgenländischen Gesellschaft*, 1887, p. 719.

with certainty get behind the idea of a *festal gathering*
for the common Semitic *ḥag*. Here then the meaning
will be "behaving as at a *ḥag* or gathering of pilgrims,"
i.e. enjoying themselves merrily[1].

Nowack is of a similar opinion; he says that the word
here can hardly mean more than "to celebrate a feast";
but he adds: "perhaps the word is originally used of the
sacred dance[2]." But apart from the question of the relationship between *ḥāgag* and *ḥūg*, if the Arabic *Ḥagg*,
"the going round in a circle," is the word from which
the Hebrew *ḥag* is derived, and presumably there is little
doubt about that, then the root-meaning of *ḥāgag* will
be "to go round in a circle," and this was the essence of
the sacred dance—or of one type of the sacred dance—
among the Semites. Wellhausen points out that the
central and most important part of the *cultus* of the
ancient Arabs was the circuit round the sanctuary, or,
when this was offered, round the sacrifice. It is from
this fact, he says, that the *Ḥagg*, which means really
"the sacred dance," is so called. He points out, further,
that this original meaning of the word has not even yet
been entirely lost in Arabic, for the verb still often has
as its transitive object the stone or the "house." The
holy stone is itself called *Davar* "the object of the encirclement" because of the custom of performing the
sacred dance round it. Evidence is forthcoming that
this was done not only round the sacred stone, the
Kaaba, but also in all sanctuaries generally[3]. König
gives as the primary meaning of *ḥāgag* "to make dancing
movements," "to turn," and regards the sense of "cele-

[1] *Notes on the Hebrew Text of the Books of Samuel*, p. 173 (1890).
[2] In "Handkommentar zum A.T.," *Die Bücher Samuelis*, p. 143 (1902).
[3] *Reste Arabischen Heidenthums*, pp. 109 f. (1897).

brating a feast" as secondary[1]. This is borne out by
the use of the word in Ps. cvii. 27, where it means "to
go round in a circle," like a drunken man.

The chief original Hebrew term for a religious dance
was doubtless *ḥag*. The rendering "feast" or "festival"
will indeed suffice in most cases, but only because religious festivals necessarily included the sacred dance,
at least as long as the sacred stones remained in the
sanctuaries[2].

There is thus sufficient justification for reckoning this
root among those which are used for "to dance" in the
Old Testament.

Then as to the root *pāsaḥ* (in its intensive form *pisseaḥ*).
According to Exod. xii. 13, 23 the root-meaning of this
word would appear to be "to spare," for we read there:
"...and when I see the blood *I will pass over* you, and
there shall be no plague upon you"; and again: "...and
when he seeth the blood upon the lintel, and on the two
side posts, Jahwe *will pass over* the door, and will not
suffer the destroyer to come into your houses to destroy
you." Both Zimmern[3] and Schrader[4] hold that the word
is derived from the Assyrian *pasâḥu*, "to pacify," which
would support the *Exodus* interpretation. Robertson
Smith, on the other hand, thinks it by no means clear
that this was the original meaning;

"there is," he says, "no certain occurrence of the name
before *Deuteronomy* (in Exod. xxxiv. 25 it looks like a
gloss), and the corresponding verb denotes some kind
of religious performance, apparently a dance, in 1 Kings
xviii. 26. A nocturnal ceremony at the consecration of

[1] *Hebräisches und Aramäisches Wörterbuch*, p. 98 (1910).
[2] *Encycl. Biblica*, I. 999.
[3] *Beiträge...*, p. 92.
[4] *Keilinschriftliche Bibliothek des A.T.*, p. 610 (3rd ed.).

a feast is already alluded to in Isa. xxx. 29, who also
perhaps alludes to the received derivation of *pāsaḥ* in
xxxi. 5[1]. But the Deuteronomic passover was a new
thing in the days, of Josiah (2 Kings xxiii. 21 f.). It
underwent further modification in the exile...[2]."
So that the opinion is worth hazarding as to whether
Pesaḥ, the Passover, did not originally get its name from
the particular form of limping dance peculiar to it, just
as the ordinary feast got its name from the sacred dance,
the *Ḥagg*, which was characteristic of it. See further
p. 92.

A ritual dance of a somewhat similar character is
mentioned in Gen. xxxii. 31, 32, where Jacob, as he passed
over Penuel, "limped upon his thigh." Here the root
used is *tzāla'*, which in this sense occurs here only[3]; but
there is the place-name *tzēla'*, Saul's ancestral home
(2 Sam. xxi. 14), which was possibly an ancient sanctuary where this special kind of limping dance was performed.

These, then, are the words used in the Old Testament
for "dancing" in its various forms; they will come before
us again and their meanings will be more fully illustrated
when we deal in the following chapters with the nature
of the sacred dance.

II

It will be appropriate if we add here a word or two
about the musical accompaniment (if this can in all
cases be called "musical") to dancing so far as can be
gathered from the Old Testament.

[1] "He will protect and deliver it, *he will pass over* and pre-
serve it."

[2] *Encycl. Britannica*, xviii. 343 *b* (9th ed.).

[3] But see Mic. iv. 6 f., Zeph. iii. 19, Jer. xx. 10, Ps. xxxv. 15,
xxxviii. 18, Job xviii. 12, from which a clear meaning of the root
is gained.

In its earliest and simplest form this accompaniment
consisted of the rhythmic beating of what is translated
"timbrel" in the Revised Version; the word is *tôph* in
Hebrew, and it was probably the most primitive instrument among the Hebrews. It would be better described
as a hand-drum, or "tom-tom," being made of a circular
(though also square and sometimes probably three-sided)
piece of wood over which the skin of an animal, after
preparation, was tightly drawn and fastened with a thin
thong of skin. It was held in one hand and struck with
the open palm of the other. In addition to this two
other instruments of percussion are mentioned as accompanying dancing, namely "cymbals," *tzeltzĕlim*, and what
are called *metziltaim*, evidently also cymbals in some
form or another as both words come from the same root;
the latter must clearly have been held one in each hand
and struck together, the dual form of the word shows
this. Wind instruments for accompaniment were represented by the *ḥalîl*, "flute," and the *'ugâb*, perhaps
something in the nature of a Pan's-pipe, though this is
quite uncertain; it is mentioned in Gen. iv. 21, where
the Revised Version renders it "pipe." Stringed instruments as an accompaniment to dancing were a later
development, though of course used in what are to us
early times, among the Israelites; the simplest of these
were the *kinnôr*, "lyre" and the *nēbel*, "harp." For the
accompaniment to dancing of all three types of instruments, percussion, wind, and string, see Job xxi. 11, 12.
We also read of "rattles," *mĕna'nĕ'im*, probably something equivalent to the *sistrum* of the Egyptians[1].

Besides instrumental, there was also vocal accompani-

[1] Cp. Nowack, *Hebräische Archäologie*, i. 273 (1894), where an
illustration of the Egyptian instrument is given.

ment, and doubtless the rhythmic clapping of hands, the most primitive form of accompaniment, and the beating of the thighs, though neither of these is mentioned in the Old Testament.

It has been truly said that

music is rarely divorced from dancing in the early stages of culture, and seldom advances beyond mere rhythm into melody or harmony. To a modern European ear it sounds not much more than rhythmic noise, a mere marking of time for concerted movement of the limbs, monotonous and unattractive, if heard without its origin and inspiration—the dance[1].

But the writer is mistaken in his mention of harmony here; such a thing was quite unknown in "the early stages of culture," if he means by that "culture" among uncivilized men[2].

The normal accompaniment to the sacred dance, then, among the Hebrews was the beating of the drum and the blowing of the flute; this, as will be seen in the following chapters, is true of all peoples. The accompaniment of stringed instruments is, as we have said, a later development.

[1] J. M. Brown, *Maori and Polynesian, their origin, history and culture*, p. 202 (1907).
[2] See the present writer's *The Psalms in the Jewish Church*, pp. 5 ff. (1910).

CHAPTER V

THE SACRED PROCESSIONAL DANCE, AND DANCES IN HONOUR OF SUPERHUMAN POWERS

I

A$_N$ illustration of the processional type of dance among the Israelites which immediately suggests itself is that of "David and all the house of Israel dancing before Jahwe with all their might" (2 Sam. vi. 5)[1]. The picture is that of an imposing procession, headed by the king going in front of the Ark into Jerusalem. The entire body of those forming the procession is described as dancing, but special attention is drawn to David, and the words used in reference to his mode of dancing are instructive; he not only dances in the ordinary sense of the word (*sāḥaq*), but he "rotates (*kārar*) with all his might" (verse 14), and "jumps" (*pāzaz*, verse 16), and "whirls round" (*ḥūl*); and in the parallel passage 1 Chron. xv. 29, his dancing is described as "skipping" (*rāqad*) or the like; it is the word used in Isa. xiii. 21 of the "hopping" of satyrs, and also of "galloping" horses (Joel ii. 5) and "jolting" chariots (Nah. iii. 2). The self-abandonment of this dancing can be imagined in the light of Michal's jibe that the king had shamelessly uncovered himself. Nevertheless, the religious character of the processional dance is obvious, and is emphasized by

---

[1] The text is clearly corrupt, but the above seems to be the best reconstruction; see Nowack, *Die Bücher Samuelis*, p. 172 (1902); the Septuagint reads lit. "with strength" (cp. 1 Chron. xiii. 8).

the phrase "before Jahwe," and by the fact that David "was girded with a linen ephod" (verse 14), the officiating priest's dress (see 1 Sam. ii. 18).

It is probable that the sacred processional dance is again referred to, though one cannot say so positively, in such passages as Ps. cxlix. 3: "Let them praise His name in the dance; let them sing praises unto Him with timbrel (*tôph*) and lyre"; cl. 4: "Praise Him with timbrel and dance," etc.; and although in Ps. lxviii. 24, 25 (25, 26 in Hebr.) there is no special mention of the dance, it is clearly implied by the reference to the damsels playing on the timbrel, which was the usual accompaniment to dancing; the passage runs: "They see Thy goings forth [*i.e.* processions in honour of Jahwe], O God, the goings forth of my God, my King, into the sanctuary; the singers go before, behind (are) those playing stringed instruments, in the midst (are) damsels playing timbrels," see also Ps. lxxxvii. 7.

Further quotations are unnecessary, for it is clear that the sacred processional dance formed a normal adjunct to worship among the Israelites.

In studying these types of the sacred dance among other peoples we are faced with the same difficulty that meets us in the case of various passages where the dance is mentioned in the Old Testament, viz. it is by no means always possible to say whether a *processional* dance is meant or not. It is, therefore, inevitable that some uncertainty should exist in the case of some of the illustrations to be offered; but if not always of the processional type, the examples to be given will all illustrate the sacred dance as an act of honour to some superhuman power.

II

As to those peoples most closely allied to the Israelites, namely the Syrians and Arabs, our *data*, so far as processional dances are concerned, are very scanty, though we are not without information on the general subject of the sacred dance among them. In one of the inscriptions found in Deir el-Ḳala near Beirut there is a reference to Θεω Βαλμαρκωδι; he is called upon as Βαλμαρκως κοίρανε κώμων; this witnesses to the existence of a Phoenician god known as *Baal-Marqôd*, according to the Semitic form, *i.e.* the "Baal, or Lord, of dancing[1]." He was either thought of as the originator of the sacred dance among the Phoenicians, just as the Greeks and others ascribed the origin of dancing to certain gods and goddesses; or else he was so called "because of a bacchanalian dance which was performed in his honour[2]"; or because he was the god, *par excellence*, to whom dancing was due as an act of homage[3]. The name shows that among the Phoenicians the sacred dance had its place.

We shall come, later on, to other types of the sacred dance among the Syrians and Arabs. Here we may, in passing, point to the fact that the Bedouin Arabs of the Syrian Desert even at the present day perform dances in honour of exalted personages; this may confidently be regarded, especially in view of other evidence to be given below, as pointing to similar dances being performed in earlier times in honour of gods; for divinities

[1] See Renan, *Mission de Phénice*, pp. 355 f. (1864); Clermont-Ganneau, *Rec. d'Arch. Or.* i. 95, 103 (1896).
[2] De la Saussaye, *Lehrbuch der Religionsgeschichte*, i. 372, 380 (3rd ed.).
[3] Robertson Smith, *Religion of the Semites*, p. 95 (1894); Lagrange, *Études sur les religions Sémitiques*, p. 84 (1903).

were honoured in this way for ages before men were. Thus Ritter describes the dancing of the Bedouin Arabs which he witnessed, adding that the far-travelled sailors who were with him told him that this mode of dancing was strikingly similar to that which they had seen performed by the savage South Sea islanders[1]. Dancing in honour of the newly married couple, regarded as king and queen, is interestingly described by Wetzstein[2]. Such dances, though not now strictly sacred, deserve a passing reference, for they have a long history behind them, and at one time were certainly connected with religion.

In many Babylonian psalms and hymns which were sung in procession, and which have come down to us, there is, it is true, no mention of dancing; but it is difficult to believe that it did not take place, especially in view of the evidence to be given below. The silence may well be due to the fact that it was so obvious a part of the ritual that there would have been no point in mentioning it. One can hardly conceive of its absence, knowing what we do of the Semitic religious temperament, during such a great festival, for example, as that of the re-entry of Marduk on the 11th Nisan into the temple of E-sagila. On this occasion a great procession of priests and choir was formed, and during the re-entry of the god into his sanctuary they sang the hymn beginning:

"O Lord, at the entering-in into thy sanctuary...[3]."

At such a time of solemn religious rejoicing it can

---

[1] *Die Erdkunde im Verhältniss zur Natur und zur Geschichte des Menschen*, xv. 729 (1850).
[2] *Zeitschrift der Deutschen morgenländischen Gesellschaft*, xxii. 105 ff. (1868); on this see further below, p. 179.
[3] See M. Jastrow, *Die Religion Babyloniens und Assyriens*, i. 503 (1905).

hardly be doubted, judging from many analogies, that some form of sacred dance formed a striking feature of the ritual. The dance-step may well have been of a sedate character, but, as we have seen, the steps and performance of the sacred dance range from an almost march-like, though rhythmical, tread to antics of the most diverse character. It is important to remember that in Assyrian the word for "to dance" (*rakâdu*) means also "to rejoice." Among all the Semites the religious festivals were special times of rejoicing. So that when we read of processions during Babylonian and Assyrian festivals it is justifiable to assume that sacred dances were performed as a recognized part of the ritual.

But we are not without tangible evidence on the subject. On an inscription discovered in the palace of Asshurbanipal a procession is depicted which is led by men playing harps; the foremost among these, each of whom has one of his legs raised, quite obviously represent dancers. They are followed by women with arms uplifted, and also by children who seem to be clapping their hands, apparently in rhythmical time with the dancers. An illustration of this is given, *e.g.*, by Jeremias[1], who quotes from the inscription the Assyrian account of Hezekiah's subjection to Sennacherib. In this inscription, among other things sent by the king of Judah to Nineveh, "playing men and women" are mentioned; the illustration represents these as both dancing and playing instruments. It is, therefore, as Jeremias rightly emphasizes, very important for the light it throws on the subject of the Temple music and worship

---

[1] *Das alte Testament im Lichte des alten Orients*, p. 307 (1904); see also Schrader, *Die Keilinschriften und das alte Testament*, pp. 45 ff. (1883).

in pre-exilic times. But it also throws light on Assyrian usage since it is obvious that the inscription reflects Assyrian ideas.

Mention may be made here, but very tentatively, of three inscriptions found in Cyprus by Ohnefalsch-Richter. It is conceivable that these bear witness, though indirectly, to early Mesopotamian ritual, for in style and representation they are somewhat reminiscent of ancient Babylonian cylinder seals. They are numbered cxxviii. 4, 5, 6 and a sacred dance is represented on each; they are cylindrical in form, and very ancient, pre-Homeric and pre-Mycenaean, according to Ohnefalsch-Richter, who says also that they bear a striking similarity to later Olympic representations[1]. The dancers wear long dresses rather like those of priests on Assyrian cylinder seals.

III

A religious processional dance of great interest is that represented on the well-known Hittite rock-inscription at Boghazkeui, in Cappadocia. The central portion of this inscription represents a company of gods and goddesses; towards them, from either side, the procession moves; the figures on the left hand which form the procession are almost exclusively men, while those on the right are all women. The men all wear the cone-shaped Hittite cap and tip-tilted shoes, and they are performing a running-step dance, the right feet being partly raised and touching the ground only with their toes. The inscription belongs approximately to B.C. 1200[2]. That it

[1] *Kypros, die Bibel, und Homer*, i. 445, and the above numbered inscriptions in vol. ii. (1893).

[2] A full illustration is given in Hommel's *Geschichte Babyloniens und Assyriens*, between pp. 270–271 (1888). A good description will also be found in Messerschmidt's "Die Hettiter," in *Der alte Orient*, iv. 23 f.; Garstang, *The Land of the Hittites*, pp. 220 ff. (1910).

represents a religious processional dance is clear both because of the presence of gods and goddesses, and also from the fact that in front of or over the heads of a number of the figures there are hieroglyphic signs which denote the names of divinities.

A small inscription on a haematite cylinder, from Cyprus, also represents a Hittite sacred processional dance. As in the previous inscription, the procession, which is preceded and followed by a priest, moves towards the god. Ohnefalsch-Richter thinks that the scene represents a moment at which the dancers are resting[1].

IV

Although we find that among the Egyptians the *data* leave something to be desired, yet they are sufficient to suggest that dancing as a religious ceremony formed an important feature among them. As is the case among all other peoples the sacred dance has divine sanction.

Hathor, for example, was the goddess of music and dancing, and is often depicted with a small boy rattling a sistrum in front of her....The king, in the capacity of Hathor's son, similarly rattles a sistrum in front of her and is called "goodly *Ihy* (the goddess's child) of the golden one of the gods."

The name *Ihwy*, a variant form of *Ihy*, is applied to the priests of Hathor; they are represented as "dancing and clattering castanets[2]." At the festivals held in honour of Hathor and Bastet dancing was an indispensable feature; so, too, at the Apis festivals[3]. Again, Bēs, or

[1] *Op. cit.* I. 446; the inscription is numbered cxxvii. 1, in vol. II.
[2] A. M. Blackman, in Hastings' *ERE*, x. 294 *b*; see also the same writer's *The Rock Tombs of Meir*, I. 22 ff., plate II (1914–15).
[3] Erman, *Aegypten und aegyptisches Leben im Alterthum*, I. 335 f. (1885).

Bēsa, originally a dancing figure of the Sudanese type, is represented on inscriptions as holding the youthful sun-god Harpokrates in his left arm, and offering him food with the right hand; he also provides for the young sun-god's amusement, and is depicted performing grotesque dances before him, and playing the harp and laughing. Thus he, too, became in course of time, a god of dance, music, and merriment[1].

In dancing in honour of their gods and goddesses, therefore, the Egyptians were employing a method of honouring which they imitated from the gods themselves; and this seems to have been the case, at one time or other, of their religious history, with most, if not all, races, so far as the evidence enables us to judge.

As to processional dances Blackman says that

there is some reason for supposing that at Thebes and elsewhere, on the occasion of the annual festival of Ḥathor, that goddess's priestesses, when the temple service and the subsequent procession were ended, paraded the streets, and, in company with the *Iḥwy*-priests, stopped at one house after another in order to bestow Ḥathor's blessing upon the inmates. This they did by dancing and singing and holding out to their audience—perhaps that they might touch them—the emblems of their goddess, the sistra and *mnit*-necklaces[2].

Again, according to Apuleius, there was a sacred dance in connexion with the worship of Isis. On stated days there was a great procession held in honour of this goddess which went through the streets of the city; the column was headed by a band of dancing masqueraders.

[1] Wiedemann, *Die Religion der alten Ägypter*, p. 87 (1890).
[2] *ERE*, xii. 780 *a*, 781 *b*; see also the same writer in the *Journal of Egyptian Archaeology*, vii. 22.

He describes this procession of the *Isidis Navigium* minutely; among other details he mentions that in one part of it there were musicians, playing on pipes and flutes, followed by a chorus of chosen youths, clad in snowy white garments; behind them came more musicians playing on pipes, and many other men jingling on bronze, silver, and even golden sistra[1].

Another kind of procession, namely of barges, in which dancing also took place, is described by Herodotus in speaking of the religious festivals of the Egyptians. He says:

Now, when they are being conveyed to the city of Bubastis, they act as follows,—men and women embark together, great numbers of both sexes in every barge; some of the women have castanets which they play, and the men play on the flute during the whole journey; the rest of the men and women sing and clap their hands together at the same time. When in the course of their passage they come to any town, they lay their barge near to the land and do as follows, some of the women do as I have described...some dance, and others stand up and pull up their clothes. This they do at every town by the river-side[2].

Mention may be here appropriately made of a kind of ritual dance, though not processional in the strict sense, which seems to be represented by a scene very often portrayed on the doors of Egyptian temples. Here the king is seen hastening towards the deity while performing a curious dance-like running step in which only the fore-part of the foot touches the ground. Kees has shown that this frequently occurring representation on

---

[1] *The Golden Ass*, XI. 8–17 (the date of Apuleius is the second half of the second century A.D.); see also Herodotus, II. 61 ff.

[2] II. 58–60.

Egyptian temple-doors does in fact record a ritual dance
in honour of the god which was performed by the king
when making his offerings[1].
Other types of the sacred dance among the Egyptians
will come before us later. It may be remarked here,
however, that, in regard to the sacred dance in general,
it was, in the more ancient periods, of a staid and
measured character, if we may judge from the inscriptions. From the time of the new empire onwards it
assumed a form more like that of modern times. As to
the apparel worn for the sacred dance and the mode of
its performance, what held good of dancing in general
applies also to this, as may be gathered, again, from the
inscriptions. In most representations the women, like
the men, wear quite short tunics, the former being decked
with all kinds of ornaments; sometimes long transparent
robes are worn, but this is exceptional. The women hold
tambourines which they strike with the open palm,
others have castanets which they click. Mostly they
appear whirling about, evidently in quick time. The
representations show that there was much bending and
other movements of body and limbs[2].

V

Among the Greeks dancing has from the earliest times
been associated with gods and goddesses. Thus, for
example, Apollo, Ares, Dionysos, Pan, are all described
as dancers. Artemis dances with her companions, and

[1] *Der Opfertanz des ägyptischen Königs*, pp. 105 ff. (1912); that
the running step was really a ritual dance is shown on pp. 109–119.
[2] Erman, *op. cit.* I. 299–337; and see further generally, Cham-
pollion, *Monuments de l'Égypte* (1844); Lepsius, *Denkmäler...*
(1897...); cp. Reinach, *Orpheus*, p. 42 (1909). As to the sacred
dancing among the *Therapeutae*, of later times, see Philo, *De Vita
Contemplativa*, pp. 127–129 in F. C. Conybeare's edition (1895).

even Zeus and Hera do not disdain it. The "Pyrrhic Dance[1]," accompanied by flute-players, which was performed during the festival of *Panathenaia*[2], was said by some to be have been invented by the Dioscuri[3], according to others it was originated by Athena. The Muses danced on the Helicon around the altar of Zeus[4]. In the train of Dionysos were the saytrs with their special dance, the *Sicinnis*[5].

That wherein the gods themselves delighted would, of course, delight their worshippers; and it is true to say that there was scarcely ever worship among the Greeks without song and dance. In his *Peri Orcheseōs* (xv. 177) Lucian says:

...I pass over the fact that you cannot find a single ancient mystery in which there is not dancing....To prove this I will not mention the secret acts of worship, on account of the uninitiated. But this much all men know, that most people say of those who reveal the mysteries, that they "dance them out[6]."

There is abundant evidence to show the truth of Farnell's

[1] Its home was Sparta; it was introduced into Athens in the sixth century B.C. in the time of Pisistratus; ultimately it became a mere war game.

[2] See A. Mommsen, *Feste der Stadt Athen*, pp. 98 ff. (1898), where details will be found; an interesting account of the great procession is given on pp. 131 ff.; see also the same author's *Heortologie*, pp. 116–205 (1864).

[3] Cp. Gruppe, *Griechische Mythologie*, I. 165, 167, II. 1198 f., etc. (1906).

[4] Hesiod, *Theog.* 259; Thucydides, IV. 3; Livy, XXVI. 9; Virgil, *Aeneid* VIII. 285; Plutarch, *Thes.* 21 (*EB*, I. 998); and see especially Emmanuel, *La Danse Grecque antique*, pp. 285 ff. (1896).

[5] On the whole subject of the worship of Dionysos see Foucart, *Le culte de Dionysos en Attique* (1906). For the dances in connexion with his worship see below, pp. 121 ff.

[6] Quoted by Andrew Lang, *Myth, Ritual and Religion*, I. 272 (1901). See also de la Saussaye, *op. cit.* II. 246.

statement that "the dance and song were indispensable in Greek religious service[1]."

This fondness of the ancient Greeks for dancing necessitated suitable places where it could be performed, whether for religious or secular purposes. Ready-made plots for this were rarely to be looked for, since what was wanted was a more or less circular level space. It happened far more frequently that the ground had to be prepared artificially[2] and a dancing-ground constructed by levelling up the soil which then had sand strewn upon it. But wear and tear, as well as the dampness of the ground, would soon have called for something more solid and abiding, and therefore pavements were laid. By means of patterns formed of differently coloured stones such pavements served also the purpose of facilitating dance-formations. Such places for dancing were a source of pride to the Greek cities in the time of Homer when there were as yet no open spaces of public resort[3].

At least two inscriptions on which the sacred processional dance is depicted have been found in Cyprus; one is a relief on limestone; it represents a procession approaching the deity before whom an altar stands; underneath on the left a sacred dance is vividly portrayed, and on the right a sacred feast is taking place[4]. The other, which is of a simpler character, shows the god seated under a tree, the worshippers are coming towards him in solemn procession[5].

[1] *The Cults of the Greek States*, ii. 472 (1909).
[2] See the first line in the quotation from the *Iliad* on p. 70.
[3] These details are from Sittl, *Archäologie der Kunst*, pp. 378 f. (1895), where much further information will be found.
[4] Ohnefalsch-Richter, *op. cit.* vol. ii, No. cxxvii. 2.
[5] *Ibid.* No. cxxviii. 3.

A great deal of light is thrown upon our subject by representations on ancient Greek pottery, etc.; from a wealth of material we select the following illustrations. On a vase-painting in the British Museum[1] a triumphal dance procession is portrayed, it is in all probability intended to be taking place in honour of Dionysos; men and women are dancing, the latter playing tambourines and lyres; in the centre is the god sitting on a camel. Some of the figures are Greek, others are clearly oriental, thus illustrating the alien character of the cult of Dionysos. The dancing in honour of this god is dealt with in Chapter VII; this example of it is given here because it illustrates the processional type of the sacred dance. Many illustrations can be seen in the British Museum, and excellent reproductions of originals are given in various books[2].

Our most informing source is, of course, Greek literature. In the examples to be given we shall not restrict ourselves to processional dances, for it is not always possible to say what formation a dance took.

Sacred dances were performed in honour of Artemis[3] at the feast of *Tithēnidia* which was celebrated in the temple of Artemis Koruthalia by a stream outside Sparta; on this occasion sucking pigs and loaves were sacrificed to the goddess. She was apparently also honoured with sacred dance on Parnassos, for Farnell refers to a passage in the *Phoenissae* according to which a maidens' chorus was danced there "in honour of the

---

[1] Cat. E, 695
[2] Such as Müller und Wieseler, *Denkmäler der alten Kunst*, see e.g. I. plate XLIV (1854...); Jane E. Harrison, *Prolegomena to the Study of Greek Religion* (1903), who gives a number of illustrations.
[3] These were sometimes of a lascivious character.

ἀθάνατος θεά, who, from the context, appears to be Artemis[1]." A passage in Pausanias runs as follows:

A third cross-road leads on the right to Caryae, and to the sanctuary of Artemis; for Caryae is sacred to Artemis and the nymphs, and an image of Artemis Caryatis stands here under the open sky. Here every year the Lacedaemonian maidens dance in troops their national dance[2].

Frazer, in his notes on the passage, says that the dancing of the Lacedaemonian maidens "is said to have been taught the Lacedaemonians by Castor and Pollux (Lucian, *De Saltatione*, 10)...." "The name Caryae," he says further, "means 'walnut-trees,' and may have been given to the town from the walnut-trees which grew there[3]." Further on Pausanias tells of the Messenians who "waylaid by day the maidens who were dancing at Caryae in honour of Artemis, and seizing the wealthiest and noblest of them, carried them off to a village in Messenia[4]." When dancing in honour of Artemis the maidens were dressed in short *chitón*, and carried a basket-like receptacle on their heads[5].

The worship of Artemis, as Curtius has observed, was peculiarly associated with low-lying land and reed-covered marshes. The reeds shared with men in the worship of the goddess, and moved to the sound of the music in her festivals, or, as Strabo says, the baskets danced, or in Laconia maidens crowned with reeds danced[6].

[1] *Op. cit.* II. 472; see also p. 463.
[2] III. x. 7 (Frazer's ed.). See further, the interesting notes in Hitzig et Bluemner's *Pausaniae Graeciae Descriptio*, I. 766 (1896).
[3] III. p. 320; see also Hitzig et Bluemner, *in loc.*; Farnell, *op. cit.* II. 472.
[4] IV. xvi. 9. It recalls the episode of the maidens of Shiloh dancing in honour of Jahwe, Judg. xxi. 19 ff.
[5] Cp. Emmanuel, *La Danse Grecque antique* (1896); for illustrations see Müller und Wieseler, *op. cit.* II. 17188 ff.
[6] Ramsay, in the *Journal of Hellenic Studies*, IV. 36 (1883).

At the Brauronian ceremonies of Artemis it was the custom for young maidens to dance, in honour of the goddess, dressed in saffron robes; in this dance both they and the priestess were called "bears." The saffron robe, according to Farnell, was "possibly worn in order to imitate the tawny skin of the bear," but he is doubtful of this; it is, however, very probable, as he says, that in the earliest times of the rite an actual bear-skin was worn by the dancers[1]. This dance was known by the name of *Arkteia*; quite young girls took part in it, from the ages of five to ten, and it appears to have been a kind of initiation by which they were consecrated to Artemis before arriving at puberty[2].

On the dance called *Orkēsis Iōnikē*, which was performed in honour of Artemis, see *Julii Pollucis Onomasticon*, IV. 193. Mention is also made of the dancing in honour of this goddess at Elis, in Pisatid territory, Pausan. VI. xxii. 1; see also Farnell, *The Cults of the Greek States*, II. 445; and for other dances belonging to her worship see Gruppe, *op. cit.* I. pp. 254, 283, 342, II. 842 and especially 1284; Lobeck, *Aglao*. II. 1085 ff.

The dancing performed at the festival of *Gymnopaediae*, also in honour of Artemis, as well as Apollo and Latona,

---

[1] Cp. Reinach, *Orpheus*, p. 123 (1909): "Les jeunes filles athéniennes, qui célèbrent le culte de l'Artémis-ourse, s'habillent en ourses et se disent des ourses."

[2] *Op. cit.* II. 436 f.; see further Gruppe, *op. cit.* II. 1284, 1293; Lobeck, *Aglaophamus*, 1086 (1829); Bekker, *Anecdota Graeca*, I. 445 (1814–21); Lübker, *Real-Lex. des Klassischen Altertums*, s.v. Artemis (1914); Hesychius, s.v. Βραυρωνίοις; Mommsen, *Feste der Stadt Athen*, pp. 456 ff.; *Heortologie*, pp. 406 ff.; and see also Pausan. I. xxiii. 7. Cp. the custom among the Azimba of east-central Africa, when maidens attain puberty they celebrate the occasion by a dance in which only women take part: see Hartland in *Anthropological Essays presented to E. B. Tylor*, p. 197 (1907).

which was held in Sparta at the beginning of July, is referred to by Pausanias; he says:

> In the market-place at Sparta there are images of Pythaean Apollo, Artemis, and Latona. This whole place is called *Chorus*, because at the festival of *Gymnopaediae*, to which the Lacedaemonians attach the greatest importance, the lads dance choral dances in honour of Apollo[1].

Gruppe draws attention to the dancing performed in honour of Apollo *Karneios*[2], so also Bekker[3]. Mention may also be made of the Cretan legend of the birth of Zeus which is represented on coins from Tralles; they have the inscription Διὸς γοναί, with Corybantes dancing in honour of the new-born god, and striking their shields[4].

There can be no doubt that *every* type of dance among the Greeks was in its origin connected with religion; but in the case of some it is evident that they quite lost their religious character. The "Pyrrhic Dance," which was at one time purely sacred and later lost this character, is an instance[5]. Another is that of the dance called the "Labyrinth," known also as the "Game of Troy," and "Ariadne's Dance[6]." Réville, in referring to it, says that in certain mythologies it has been observed that all the stars move, turning round the earth and following their regular courses. Nothing more is wanted for these movements of the stars to be likened to a rhythmic and complicated dance. The consequence will be a religious dance in honour of the "army of the heavens." The dance will develop in a manner apparently entangled, but

---

[1] iii. xi. 7.
[2] *Op. cit.* i. 162. Herodotus refers to the Carneian festival in vii. 206.
[3] *Op. cit.* i. 234.   [4] Gruppe, *op. cit.* i. 271.
[5] For its religious character see Mommsen, *Heortologie*, pp. 163 ff.
[6] See further, p. 71, and W. H. Matthews, *Mazes and Labyrinths*, pp. 19 ff., 156 ff. (1922).

nevertheless methodical. There were several sacred dances having this character of imitation of the movements of the stars; among others, that of the "Labyrinth," which was danced in Crete and Delos. The labyrinth itself, with its thousand circuits, was a symbol of the starry heaven, and the dance of the same name must have been a sort of animated representation of it[1].

An interesting representation of this dance occurs on an Etruscan Polledrara vase, painted by an Ionian artist, and found in Cyprus, where the dance was at one time performed in Amathus in honour of Aphrodite-Ariadne; according to tradition Theseus led the Attic youths and maidens in this dance[2]. The representation is superbly executed. The connexion of the name of Ariadne with this dance is sufficient to show its originally religious character, and probably it remained so always, theoretically; but even as early as the time of Homer, according to the following account from the *Iliad*, the religious element does not appear prominently:

Also with cunning art he wrought a dancing-floor; like unto that which erst, in broad Knossos, Daidalos had made for fair-haired Ariadne. Thereon young men and comely damsels were dancing, that clasped each other by the wrist. The damsels were arrayed in vestures of fine linen, and the men in fine-spun tunics, glossy with oil. And the damsels wore fair coronals, while the men carried golden dirks hanging from baldrics of silver. Now they would dance with cunning feet, lightly, as when a potter sitting at his task maketh trial of the wheel that is ready to his hands, to see if it run; now they would dance in long lines, facing one another. And a great company stood around the beauteous dancing-

---

[1] *Prolegomena of the History of Religions*, p. 123 (1884).
[2] Ohnefalsch-Richter, *op. cit.* i. 446, 448, and numbered cxxxii. 2.

place, rejoicing; and two tumblers, leading the dance, kept whirling through the midst[1].

This dance was adopted by the Romans from the Greeks. Virgil compares its complicated evolutions with the windings of the Cretan labyrinth[2]; and

that the comparison is more than a mere poetical flourish appears from a drawing on a very ancient Etruscan vase found at Tragliatella. The drawing represents a procession of seven beardless warriors dancing, accompanied by two armed riders on horseback, who are also beardless. An inscription proves that the scene depicted is the "Game of Troy"; and attached to the procession is a figure of the Cretan labyrinth, the pattern of which is well known from coins of Cnossus, on which it is often represented. The same pattern, identified by an inscription, *Labyrinthus, hic habitat Minotaurus*, is scratched on a wall at Pompeii, and it is also worked in mosaic on the floor of Roman apartments, with the figures of Theseus and Minotaur in the middle[3].

After pointing out the widespread occurrence of this labyrinth pattern, both for the purpose of games as well as of decorations, Frazer continues:

A dance or game which has thus spread over Europe, and survived in a fashion to modern times must have been very popular, and bearing in mind how often with the decay of old faiths the serious rites and pageants of grown people have degenerated into the sports of children, we may reasonably ask whether "Ariadne's Dance," or the "Game of Troy," may not have had its origin in religious ritual. The ancients connected it with Cnossus and the Minotaur. Now we have reason to hold, with many other scholars, that Cnossus was the seat of a great worship of the sun, and that the Minotaur was

[1] xviii. 590–606 (Blakeney's translation).
[2] *Aen.* v. 545–603.
[3] Frazer, *GB*, *The Dying God*, pp. 76 f. (1911).

a representative or embodiment of the sun-god. May
not, then, "Ariadne's Dance" have been an imitation of
the sun's course in the sky? And may not its intention
have been, by means of sympathetic magic, to aid the
luminary to run his race on high?...If there is any truth
in this conjecture it would seem to follow that the sinuous
lines of the labyrinth which the dancers followed in their
evolutions may have represented the ecliptic, the sun's
apparent annual path in the sky. It is some confirmation of this view that on the coins of Cnossus the sun
or a star appears in the middle of the labyrinth, the
place which on other coins is occupied by the Minotaur[1].

Frazer's interesting suggestion points to the originally
religious character of "Ariadne's Dance," which in
course of time it lost. Like the dances at Harvest and
Vintage festivals, "Ariadne's Dance" was one of the
mediums whereby the sacred dance developed into a
purely secular amusement. The same may be said of
the *Geranos*, or "Crane Dance," danced at Delos, which
was apparently derived from "Ariadne's Dance[2]"; and
also of the *Hormos*, or "Chain Dance," which was also
performed by youths and maidens holding their hands
in a changing line[3].

Finally, reference may be made to a few representations of the sacred dance found in Cyprus, in addition
to those already mentioned. On a vase, numbered
cxxxii. 1 by Ohnefalsch-Richter[4], a dance is represented
in which men and women are taking part, two of the
former hold semi-circular instruments with which they
accompany the dance; also, three of the men, one of
whom seems to be acting as the leader, carry small

[1] *GB, The Dying God*, p. 77.
[2] See Plutarch, *Theseus*, xxi.
[3] Cp. the "Ladies' Chain" in modern dancing.
[4] *Op. cit.*, and see also vol. i. 446.

swords at their sides; this illustrates the words of Homer in the quotation given above (lines 597–8). Again, on two bronze vases, numbered cxxix. 2 and cxxx. 1, the dance represented shows women only, some of whom are playing instruments, pipe, harp, and drum[1]; a similar representation occurs on a painted Etruscan vase (cxxxii. 4), while on a thin golden plate from a grave near Corinth[2] women are portrayed dancing and clothed with long garments; this is numbered xxv. 15.

VI

In turning now to the sacred dance among the Romans we find that there is not nearly the amount of material from which to gather information that there is among the Greeks. Cicero said: "No man who is in a sober state and not demented would dance either privately or in decent company[3]." If, as we may suppose was the case, this reflected the general opinion, one can well understand why it was that dancing never played such a part in the national life of the Romans as it did in that of the Greeks. Cicero, however, as is clear from the context of this quotation, was referring to dancing as a pastime, which respectable Romans regarded as inconsistent with their dignity. The dance in worship was a different matter. Nevertheless, even in this domain it did not play the part, nor anything like it, that it did among the Greeks. And what there was of it was, in the main, due to Greek influence[4]. Not altogether, however; and the influence of oriental cults must not be

---

[1] Ohnefalsch-Richter, *op. cit.* i. 448.
[2] Now in the Berl. Mus. Antiquarium.
[3] *Pro Murena*, vi. 13, quoted by Bender, *Rom und römisches Leben im Alterthum*, p. 452 (1880).
[4] Cp. Wissowa, *Religion und Kultus der Römer*, i. 382 (1902).

74 PROCESSIONAL DANCE AND DANCES

overlooked. Reinach, in speaking of the effect that
eastern religions produced upon that of Rome, pointedly
contrasts the hypocrisy of the sceptical priests in Italy
("deux aruspices, disait Coton, ne peuvent se regarder
sans rire") with the earnestness and sincerity of the
oriental priest:

> Quelle différence avec le prêtre oriental qui va droit
> au fidèle, l'appelle son frère et le traite en conséquence,
> éveille et nourrit les élans de sa dévotion, lui enseigne
> l'exstase, l'espérance d'un monde meilleur....

Then he refers to the alien influences on the religion of
Rome:

> Juvénal se plaint que l'Oronte de Syrie se soit déversé
> dans le Tibre; il aurait pu en dire autant du Nil, du
> Jourdain, et de l'Halys...L'Empire romain se remplit
> des adorateurs d'Attis, d'Isis, d'Osiris, de Sérapis, de
> Sabazios, de Zeus Dolichenos, de Mithra. Les pratiques
> les plus étranges, empreinte d'un sombre mysticisme,
> remplacèrent les froides et sévères coutumes romaines[1].

But while giving due weight to the effect of these
oriental influences, the fact remains that it is chiefly to
Greece that Rome owed the entry of new cults. Within
the small domain with which we are specially concerned
we have already considered the example of the "Game
of Troy," where it was evident that this was borrowed
from Greece. Another example which may be cited is
the ritual which accompanied the processions of supplication; a solemn dance-step was characteristic of these;
such, for instance, was that which went from the temple
of Apollo before the *Porta Carmentalis* to that of *Juno
Regina* on the Aventine; to her an offering of two white

---

[1] *Op. cit.* pp. 154 f.; cp. Warde Fowler, *ERE*, x. 820 a; Marquardt, *Das Privatleben der Römer*, p. 118 (1886); Dill, *Roman
Society in the last century of the Roman Empire*, pp. 76 ff. (1910).

cows was made by the *Decemviri*. These latter formed the centre of the procession, and in front of them were twenty-seven virgins who had to sing in honour of Juno. The singing took place during a halt in the *forum*; here the maidens sang their song while dancing with a measured, stately tread. As Wissowa says, the entire ritual was Greek from beginning to end[1]. It is probable that the dancing priests who belonged to the early Roman *cultus*[2] witness also to Greek influence.

An interesting case of what may well have been an indirect importation from Greece, and which records one of the earliest instances of the sacred dance among the Romans, is mentioned by Frazer:

"In the fourth century before our era," he writes, "the city of Rome was desolated by a great plague which raged for three years, carrying off some of the highest dignitaries and a great multitude of common folk. The historian who records the calamity informs us that when a banquet had been offered to the gods in vain, and neither human counsels nor divine help availed to mitigate the violence of the disease, it was resolved for the first time in Roman history to institute dramatical performances as an appropriate means of appeasing the wrath of the celestial powers. Accordingly, actors were fetched from Etruria, who danced certain simple and decorous dances to the music of a flute. But even this novel spectacle failed to amuse or touch, to move to tears or laughter, the sullen gods[3]...."

The means which were subsequently found to be effective do not concern us here; the point is that the sacred dance was imported from Etruria, and it is well known

[1] *Op. cit.* i. 360.
[2] Cp. Marquardt, *Das Privatleben der Römer*, p. 118, and the reff. there given (1886).
[3] *GB, The Scapegoat*, p. 65 (1913), from Liv. vii. 1–3.

that the Etruscans were largely indebted to Greece for their religious ideas and ritual.

It will be unnecessary to offer further illustrations of this type of religious dance among the Romans since it was mainly derived from Greece, and we have already devoted a section to the rite among the Greeks. It only remains to be said that there is a marked difference in the mode of performing the sacred dance between the two peoples. Due largely to national temperament, but also to earlier oriental influences, the Greeks in their sacred dances gave freer vent to natural impulse, a characteristic which was especially pronounced in the ecstatic dance, with which we deal below (pp. 119 ff.). The Romans, on the other hand, were far more restrained and dignified in their performance of them. Nevertheless, among both peoples the sacred dance was a necessary adjunct to worship, and that is the point with which we are specially concerned.

VII

We do not propose to deal, excepting incidentally, with the sacred dance among the Asiatic peoples; firstly, because it would greatly increase the bulk of this volume; and secondly, because it is doubtful whether our doing so would really throw much further light on the subject than we gain from the study of its prevalence among the peoples here considered. It may be said generally, that the Asiatics are like the other peoples with whom we deal in their belief that the sacred dance comes from the higher powers. Among them, too, the sacred dance is an important part of the ritual of worship, it has different purposes, and it is very widespread. That much even a superficial knowledge of the religion of the Asiatic peoples makes clear.

In referring to the subject of Vedic and Brahman worship in India Lehmann says that the original character of Vedic sacrifice was a friendly feast for the gods, and among the different ways of showing honour to the exalted guests during the sacrifices were offerings of incense, music, and dances, which were believed to give them pleasure[1].

VIII

Lastly, we come to consider a few examples of the sacred dance in general among some of the uncultured races.

The Dakotahs perform a sacred dance in connexion with their worship of the sun; it is executed by two young men "in a very singular attitude," as Schoolcraft says. These two young worshippers perform the dance while in a state of almost complete nudity; each has a small whistle in his mouth with which he accompanies the dance at intervals, and each faces the sun while dancing, that is, as long as the sun is above the horizon. The mode of dancing is a kind of hitch of first one leg and then the other; they do this in a rhythmic manner and keep time by beating on raw hides of parchment.... This dance is kept up for two, and occasionally three, days, during which time the worshippers partake of no food[2].

[1] In de la Saussaye, *Lehrbuch der Religionsgeschichte*, ii. 33, cp. 149 (1905), and Reinach, *Orpheus*, p. 89. A great deal of information will be found scattered about in various volumes of the *Sacred Books of the East* series, *e.g.* i, xv (Upanishads); xii, xxvi, xli, xliii, xliv (Satapatha-Brâhmana); xxxiv, xxxviii, xlviii (the Vedânta-Sûtras); xlix (Buddhist Mahâyâna Texts); xxiii, xxxi (the Zend-Avesta); xxvii, xxviii, xl (the Sacred Books of China). Also the relevant articles, which are many, in *ERE*, where special literature in abundance will be found.

[2] Schoolcraft, *The Indian Tribes of the United States*, i. 191 (ed. by F. S. Drake, 1891); there is an illustration given of this dance.

To take, next, an example from Central America; Lumholtz[1] relates of the Tarahumare Indians of Mexico that they believe that by dancing they are able to gain the favour of their gods; their dancing is "a series of monotonous movements, a kind of rhythmical exercise," which they keep up sometimes for two nights. "By dint of such hard work they think to prevail upon the gods to grant their prayers." According to the same writer, the Tarahumares say that the animals taught them how to dance; that is an interesting point which will come before us again in a moment. They regard dancing as a very serious and ceremonious matter, it is "a kind of worship and incantation rather than amusement." The same is true of the ancient Peruvians, to take a South American example; the sacred dance was the "grand form of religious demonstration among them," and they were very assiduous in this form of devotion[2].

The belief of the Tarahumares that the animals first taught them how to dance is interesting, for although it points to a relatively low religious mentality, it is a stage in advance, for example, of that of the natives of Ponape, one of the Caroline islands, in the Pacific; among these

the different families suppose themselves to stand in a certain relation to animals, and especially to fishes, and believe in their descent from them. They actually name these animals "mothers"; the creatures are sacred to the family and may not be injured. Great dances, accom-

---

[1] *Unknown Mexico*, I. 330 f. (1903).
[2] For the religious dance among the ancient Peruvians see Réville, *Hibbert Lectures*, pp. 224 ff. (1895); J. G. Müller, *Amerikanische Urreligion*, p. 385 (1867); Reinach, *Orpheus*, p. 230 (1909).

panied with the offering of prayers, are performed in their honour[1].

These animals are their gods whom they honour by dancing; the Tarahumares have separated their gods from the animals, but we may well surmise that in an earlier stage among them their gods were the animals who taught them to dance, and in whose honour they danced. Réville is certainly right in his conjecture that the sacred dance among uncultured races was the earliest form of adoration[2].

A good illustration of the way in which similar forms of worship are in vogue among different peoples where there can be no question of borrowing is afforded by the worship of the Pleiades. This was practised by the ancient Peruvians[3], though whether dancing was performed in their honour (which was highly probable) we are not told; but the aborigines of Australia "sing and dance to gain the favour of the Pleiades" (whom they call *Mormodellick*), they are worshipped as the givers of rain[4]. The Blackfeet Indians of North America likewise worship the Pleiades;

[1] Hahl, *Mittheilungen über Sitten und rechtliche Verhältnisse auf Ponape*, in "Ethnologisches Notizblatt," II. ii. 1 (1901), quoted by Frazer, *Folk-lore in the Old Testament*, I. 40 (1918). The Maoris attributed the origin of dancing to two goddesses, Raukata-uri and Raukata-mea, J. Macmillan Brown, *Maori and Polynesian*, p. 208 (1907); see also the interesting illustrations in Caillot, *Les Polynésiens orientaux...*, Pls. XLVII, XLIX–LII (1909).

[2] *Les religions des peuples non-civilisés*, pp. 251 f. (1883).

[3] Réville, *Hibbert Lectures*, p. 194.

[4] Frazer, *GB, Spirits of the Corn and of the Wild*, I. 307, 309 ff. (1912). The supremely important rôle assigned to the sacred dance among the natives of Australia is well known; see Spencer, *Native Tribes of the Northern Territory of Australia*, pp. 32, 106, 139 ff., 173, and the illustrations on p. 186 (1914); Howitt, *The Native Tribes of South-east Australia*, pp. 330, 416 (1904); Brough Smith, *The Aborigines of Victoria*, I. 166 ff. (1878), cp. Reinach, *Orpheus*, pp. 228 f.

at the general meeting of the nation there is a dance of
warriors, which is supposed to represent the dance of
the seven young men who are identified with the
Pleiades. For the Indians say that the seven stars of
the constellation were seven brothers, who guarded by
night the field of sacred seed and danced round it to
keep themselves awake during the long hours of darkness[1].

Frazer has collected many instances of the worship of
this constellation in lands widely separated; in most
cases there is no mention of dancing in its honour, but
it is difficult to believe that this did not take place during
the celebration of the Festivals held at its appearance[2].
Finally, one or two examples of the sacred dance in
the continent of Africa may be offered. Speaking of the
religion of the African aborigines generally, Schneider
says that a living faith in a beneficent god of some kind
is one of its characteristics. He is worshipped, on the
one hand, from fear; but on the other, as a mark of
gratitude; and one of the chief ways whereby this gratitude is shown is by songs and dances accompanied by
music[3]. Again, the Kaffirs perform ceremonious dances
on all sacred occasions; their mimic dances, performed
with a view to prepare for hunting or war, have also a
serious side[4]. The same is true of the Namaquas; among
these when anyone embraces Christianity it is said that
"he has given up dancing[5]." The Masai worship the god
Engai whom they conceive as embodied in the sky, or

[1] *GB, Spirits of the Corn...*, I. 311.
[2] See the whole of the Note on "The Pleiades in Primitive
Calendars," *GB, Spirits of the Corn...*, I. 307–319.
[3] W. Schneider, *Die Religion der Afrikanischen Naturvölker*,
p. 100 (1891).
[4] Fritsch, *Die Eingeborenen Süd-Afrika's*, p. 91 (1872).
[5] Fritsch, *op. cit.* p. 352.

at all events as dwelling there; he, too, is worshipped with songs and dances[1].

Examples could, of course, be multiplied to any extent; those given are, however, quite sufficient for our purpose; and, as will have been noticed, they represent, apart from Europe, all the continents.

*   *   *   *

SUMMARY AND CONSIDERATIONS

The sacred dance among the Israelites was performed in honour of Jahwe, their national God; and it is evident that the processional form of dance was a normal mode in the ritual of worship. Although the evidence as to the existence of this rite among the Syrians and Arabs is scanty, yet its prevalence is sufficiently attested by the mention on an inscription of Baal-Marqôd, "the lord of dancing"; this name may well point to the belief among the Phoenicians that its divine bearer was the originator of the sacred dance; so that in performing it his worshippers did it in imitation of him, and therefore in his honour. Dances performed by the Bedouin Arabs of the Syrian Desert in honour of exalted personages may quite reasonably be regarded as an adaptation of the earlier religious rite of dancing in honour of a god or spirit.

Religious processions which were common in the worship of Assyrians and Babylonians must be regarded as a form of sacred dance in the extended use of the term. In connexion with the well-known joyful character of the religious festivals among the Semites it is worth remembering that the Assyrian word *rakâdu* means both "to rejoice" and "to dance"; where there was rejoicing, whether of a secular or religious kind, there

---

[1] W. Schneider, *op. cit.* pp. 89 f.

was dancing; from which we may assume that at Assyrian religious festivals the sacred dance had its place. Direct evidence of the processional dance among the Assyrians is offered by an inscription found in the palace of Asshurbanipal. Some inscriptions found in Cyprus may possibly reflect Babylonian and Assyrian usage, but the dance represented on these is of a less formal character than the processional dance.

Two inscriptions, one from Boghazkeui, the other from Cyprus, bear unmistakable evidence of the religious processional dance among the Hittites.

Dancing in honour of Egyptian divinities is well attested on inscriptions; there is justification for the contention that the Egyptians believed that their gods and goddesses danced, and that therefore their worshippers performed the sacred dance in imitation of them. Hathor, Bastet, Bēs, and Isis are Egyptian divinities in connexion with whom dancing is mentioned. A special ritual dance was performed by Egyptian kings in honour of the god when making their offerings.

Of particular interest is the sacred dance among the Greeks. They, too, believed that gods and goddesses first danced; it was in honour of them, and in imitation of what they did, that their worshippers danced. Apollo, Ares, Pan, Zeus, Hera, the Dioscuri, Athena, and, above all, Dionysos and Artemis are the deities especially mentioned in this connexion. The evidence, which is abundant, is obtained from representations on pottery and inscriptions, as well as from literary sources. Among the Greeks the type of dances here considered was performed primarily in honour of gods and goddesses; but there is reason to believe that some dances had originally other purposes. "Ariadne's Dance" is probably the most striking example; for there are distinct indications of its having been at one time an imitation of the sun's course in the sky, and of having, by means of imitative magic, the purpose of assisting the sun in running its course. The Romans were primarily indebted to the Greeks for their sacred dances, though oriental influences were also pronounced.

The sacred dance was an important element in Vedic and Brahman worship; it was, likewise, performed primarily in honour of divinities.

Probably the most instructive area in which to study the sacred dance and its objects is that of the uncultured races, for among them it is seen in its native simplicity, unaffected, for the most part, by the exigencies of a more advanced civilization. The dance in honour of the sun, performed, for example, by the Dakotahs in a practically nude state points to the belief of the sun being a person with whom it was possible to have a more or less direct contact; the sensation upon the naked body of the warmth of its rays would denote this contact. The long-continued dance in its honour offers an example of touching, if *naïve*, devotion, emphasized by the accompanying fast. The belief that by means of dancing in honour of the gods they can be prevailed upon to answer prayers—as exemplified by Central American Indians—reveals a mentality so deeply ingrained in human nature that the underlying idea can be paralleled by the religious exercises of people among the most civilized nations at the present day. That is an interesting phenomenon about which much could be said, but which would involve our straying far away from the immediate subject in hand.

These same Central American Indians say that the animals taught them to dance; this belief is undoubtedly the explanation of the form of many dances in vogue among savages; just as more civilized peoples, such, for example, as the Greeks, imitated what they believed to be the dances of their gods and goddesses, so these savages imitated what they saw to be the movements of animals[1]. There, however, the parallel ceases, for the savages believed they were descended from these animals; it was, thus, their ancestors whom they honoured by their imitative dances. Could the beliefs of these Mexican Indians have developed spontaneously, untouched by extraneous influences—a thing which is, of course, out of the question now—it is quite possible that from these animals "high gods" would have been evolved. Perhaps an illustration of this evolutionary process is to be seen in one of the forms of the Greek worship of Artemis, viz. in that of the Brauronian ceremonies. The high probability that in the dance performed during these ceremonies it was at one time customary for the dancers to wear bear-skins points to the connexion of Artemis with the bear. The meaning of this ritual is clear if we suppose that some remote ancestors of the Greeks danced in honour of the bear in the belief that they were descended from bears. The dance in bear-skins would thus be a personating of the goddess, that is to say, a means of union with her[2].

Another line in the process of religious evolution is seen in the widespread worship of the Pleiades. Australian aborigines dance in their honour for the purpose of in-

[1] For other dances in imitation of animals, see Ling Roth, *The Aborigines of Tasmania*, pp. 138 ff. (1899).

[2] Cp. the personating of spirits or legendary animals among the N. American Indians, Frazer, *GB, The Scapegoat*, p. 375.

ducing them to give rain, without, apparently, forming any ideas as to the nature of the Pleiades; but the Blackfeet Indians of North America imitate in dance seven young men, identified with the Pleiades, who appear to be the guardians of the crops.

In the few examples of worship among different African aborigines given above we have seen that dancing was in honour of their gods and an essential part of their worship, and we may well believe that the reason of this was the belief that the worshippers were imitating their gods in doing so. While the purpose is always honorific, we may be sure that they also had practical ends in view, viz. either the obtaining of food, or effecting union with the god. So that it is true to say that the sacred dance was the means of satisfying two essential needs of man: natural and spiritual sustenance.

In asking, finally, what is the bearing of this short investigation upon the religion of the Israelites we note first of all that the Israelites were at one with practically all the nations of antiquity, as well as with the uncivilized peoples, in performing the sacred dance in their worship. The primary object was, among the Israelites, as among the others, to honour their God. *Why* this rite should have been thought of as pleasing to the deity we have already considered. It is, however, improbable that the question troubled the Israelites; it was sufficient that it had been handed down from time immemorial as an essential constituent in the ritual of worship.

Further, we have seen that there was a very widespread belief that the sacred dance originated with the gods, or, in the case of savages, with animals regarded as ancestors. While there is no hint in the Old Testament of any similar belief among the Israelites, we may well ask, in view of what has just been said about the ubiquity of the sacred dance itself, whether such a belief, or the echo of it, may not actually have existed among them. It can scarcely be without significance that we get definite traces of it in the later Jewish literature which preserves in such numberless instances ancient traditions. It is said, for example, in the Midrash *Shir ha-Shirim* to vii. 1 that God Himself will lead the dance of the righteous in the world to come. In an exegetical exercise of a typically Rabbinical type on Ps. xlviii. 13, 14 (14, 15 in Hebr.) we are told that the words: "Mark well her bulwarks," should be rendered: "Direct your heart to the dance"; for instead of *lĕḥēlah* one must read *lĕḥūlah* ("to the dance"). It is said, further, that, in that day the righteous shall point with their fingers and say, "This is our God, who will lead us," *i.e.* in the dance. Then it is said that the last word of the psalm *'al-muth* ("unto death") should be read *'alamôth* ("maidens"), *i.e.* God will lead the dance of the righteous in the world to come just as the maidens lead the dance in this world! We are not concerned with the exegesis, but only with the idea put forth. It is quite conceivable that some old-world tradition lies behind it. In any case, it suggests a parallel to the belief of many other peoples. It shows also that we may at times be justified in seeking for side-lights upon the religion of Israel from quarters which may not appear promising; we fully realize the pitfalls into which we may stumble in such cases, and the consequent need of caution; but one must be venturesome on occasion.

We drew attention just now to the belief of the Central American Indians that their gods could be prevailed

upon to answer prayer by means of the sacred dance;
the "limping" dance of the prophets of Baal had a
similar purpose, though in this case there is a toning
down inasmuch as there is an appeal to the pity of the
god. Not very far removed from this is the idea of
putting compulsion upon the god; an idea familiar to
uncivilized man[1]; and it is quite possible that in some
cases the sacred dance was believed to have the effect
of coercing the god to do what was required of him.
The underlying idea is similar to that expressed in
Gen. xxviii. 20–22:

And Jacob vowed a vow, saying, If God will be with
me, and will keep me in this way that I go, and will give
me bread to eat, and raiment to put on, so that I come
again to my father's house in peace, then shall Jahwe be
my God...

[1] See, *e.g.*, *GB, The Magic Art*, I. 302 ff.

CHAPTER VI

THE RITUAL DANCE ROUND
A SACRED OBJECT

I

THE ritual encircling dance, whether in procession with measured tread or in the form of a dance-step—and both are varieties of what is essentially the same thing—is perhaps the commonest kind of sacred dance. Its occurrence is world-wide. The object around which it takes place was in most cases, at any rate originally, a sacred one: an idol, an altar, a sacrificial victim, a holy tree, or a well. The encirclement was also performed round other things; but in these cases the dance is of another type to which attention will be drawn later.

Of sacred trees[1] and wells[2] among the Israelites we have abundant witness in the Old Testament; there is also plenty of evidence of their existence among other Semitic peoples, see, for example, Baudissin, *Studien zur Semitischen Religionsgeschichte*, II. 154 ff. (1876); Robertson Smith, *The Religion of the Semites*, Lecture v (1894); Lagrange, *Études sur les religions sémitiques*, pp. 158 ff., 162 ff. (1903), to mention but three of the foremost authorities. The Old Testament nowhere mentions any details of the cult in connexion with these sacred objects,

---

[1] *E.g.* Gen. xii. 6 f., xiii. 18, xiv. 13, xxxv. 4, 8; Josh. xxiv. 26; Judg. ix. 37; Jer. ii. 20, iii. 6, 13, xvii. 2; Ezek. vi. 13; Hos. iv. 13; cp. Isa. i. 29.

[2] *E.g.* Gen. xiv. 7, xvi. 14; cp. xxi. 19, 33; Josh. xv. 7, xviii. 17, xix. 8.

for reasons which have been pointed out[1], and therefore there is no allusion to the dance around them; but as we know from so many sources that wherever sacred trees and springs existed (which has been all the world over) part of the ritual in connexion with them consisted of the sacred dance, we need not gather from the silence of the Old Testament that it did not take place.

An interesting instance may be given of the way in which we are able to supplement an Old Testament record from other sources. In Num. xxi. 17, 18, occurs this song to the well:

> Spring up, O well. Sing ye unto it;
> To the well which the princes digged,
> Which the nobles of the people delved,
> With the wand, and with their staves.

Here we have a song to the well, though no mention is made of the sacred dance; but in a striking parallel, recorded by Nilus, we are told that when the nomadic Arabs found a well they danced by it and sang songs to it[2]. Both song and dance were sacred, for, as Robertson Smith says:

Of all inanimate things that which has the best marked supernatural associations among the Semites is flowing (or, as the Hebrews say, "living") water...and sacred wells are among the oldest and most ineradicable objects of reverence among all the Semites, and are credited with oracular powers and a sort of volition by which they receive or reject offerings. Of course these superstitions often take the form of a belief that the sacred spring is the dwelling-place of beings which from time to time emerge from it in human or animal form, but the funda-

---

[1] See above, pp. 33 ff.
[2] *Patrol. Graec.* (Migne), LXXIX. Col. 648.

mental idea is that the water itself is the living organism of a demoniac life, not a mere dead organ[1].

Kazwini[2] relates that "when the water [of the wells of Ilabistan] failed, a feast was held at the source, with music and dancing, to induce it to flow again." One thinks of the "Well of Fair Dances" at Eleusis; though not offering a parallel to what has just been said, it is in so far an analogy in that it was a spring at which sacred dancing took place, in this case by women in honour of Demeter[3].

We have mention of sacred dancing, again, in another connexion, viz. around the Golden Calf. The passage is Exod. xxxii. 5, 6, 19:

And when Aaron saw this, he built an altar before it; and Aaron made proclamation and said, Tomorrow shall be a feast (*ḥag*) to Jahwe. And they rose up early on the morrow, and offered burnt offerings, and brought peace offerings; and the people sat down to eat and drink, and rose up to dance[4]....And it came to pass, as soon as he [*i.e.* Moses] came nigh unto the camp, that he saw the calf and the dancing....

This definite mention of the sacred dance here justifies the assumption that it was also performed in honour of a similar idol set up in other sanctuaries, such as those in Dan and Bethel (1 Kings xii. 28, 29, 2 Kings x. 29; cp. Hos. x. 5), in Samaria (Hos. viii. 5, 6), and possibly in Gilgal (Hos. xii. 11 [12], Am. v. 4, 5)[5].

---

[1] *Rel. of the Semites*, pp. 135 f.

[2] i. 189. Quoted by Buchanan Gray, *Numbers* (Intern. Crit. Com.), pp. 288 f. (1903).

[3] Cp. Jane E. Harrison, *Prolegomena to the Study of Greek Religion*, p. 127 (1903).

[4] A reading based on the Samaritan and the Septuagint.

[5] The name "calf," *ʿēgel*, instead of "bull" or "cow," refers to its smallness (perhaps in irony). Such images could not have been

Again, there are several passages in which the encirclement of the altar is mentioned; these merit a little attention. In 1 Sam. xvi. 11, where there is, however, a little uncertainty about the reading, there is some justification in translating the Hebrew thus: "And Samuel said...we will not go round, *i.e.* the altar, till he come." The Revised Version follows the Septuagint and the Vulgate in rendering: "We will not sit down, *i.e.* to the feast, till he come"; but this use of the word is otherwise unknown in the Old Testament[1]. Taking it in its natural sense the word would here refer to the ceremonial encircling of the altar which is mentioned elsewhere in the Old Testament, and was a recognized part of the ritual in offering sacrifices among other peoples. In Ps. xxvi. 6 it is said: "I will wash mine hands in innocency and will go round thy altar, Jahwe"; this points clearly to the ritual encircling of the altar, and the incidental mention of it without further comment seems to imply that it formed part of the ordinary ritual[2]. A procession on a larger scale may well be in the mind of the writer of Ps. xlviii. 13 [12 in R.V.]: "Encompass ye Zion, and go round about her"; the context points to the reference being to some act of ritual worship; and that it is a literal, and not a figurative, encirclement that is meant

large as they were made of precious metal. But even when made of other materials, such as clay, they were small, to judge from the specimens found on the site of ancient Gezer.

[1] It is true that the word is used of "surrounding" a table in the Hebrew of Ecclus. xxxv. 1 (xxxii. 1 in Greek), but it would be precarious to cite this late Hebrew meaning of it in support of the R.V. rendering of the word in 1 Sam. xvi. 11. In Ecclus. ix. 9 it is used of "mingling" strong drink.

[2] Cp. Robertson Smith, *The Religion of the Semites*, p. 340, note 2: "The festal song of praise (*tahlil*) properly goes with the dance round the altar (cp. Ps. xxvi. 6 sq.), for in primitive times song and dance are inseparable."

is clear both from the use of *sābab*, as well as of *nāqaph*, which refers often to the surrounding of cities. An interesting passage is Ps. cxviii. 27, though there is some uncertainty again about the text. The R.V. reads: "Bind the sacrifice with cords, even unto the horns of the altar." The word *ḥag* is here translated "sacrifice"; but this is not justified (in spite of Mal. ii. 3), for, as Briggs rightly points out, the procedure "would not be in accord with sacrificial laws and usage[1]." On the other hand, to translate it by "sacred dance" would be to give the word, as we have seen, its essential meaning[2]. Then, further, the word rendered "bind" (*'asar*) can equally well mean "join"; cp. this meaning of the word in 1 Kings xx. 14, "Who will join battle?" The same use is found in 2 Chron. xiii. 3, "And Abijah joined battle"; in each case this root (*'asar*) is used. So that our passage could be rendered quite correctly: "Join the sacred dance." As to the word translated "cords," or "ropes," this would be used quite appropriately in connexion with dancing; it is the same idea as that connected with *ḥebel* ("chain," or "band"), used of prophets going about in single file (see further below,

[1] *Psalms* (Intern. Crit. Com.), II. 408 (1907).
[2] Cp. Job xxvi. 10: "He hath worked out a circle (*ḥôq ḥāg*) upon the face of the waters"; or perhaps better: "He hath circumscribed a boundary...." This illustrates the root meaning of *ḥag*, "a circle"; and this is the formation of the festival dance. See, further, Driver and Gray, *Job*, Part II, Philological Notes, pp. 154, 180 (1921); Budde, *Hiob*, p. 146 (1896); Ball, *The Book of Job*, p. 322 (1922). See also Prov. viii. 27, and cp. Isa. xix. 17: "And the land of Judah shall be for a reeling (*ḥagga'*) to Egypt," *i.e.* Egypt will become giddy through fear at the sight of Judah, and will thus "reel." *Ḥagga'* "may either be from an original sense of *ḥāgag*, or it may be equivalent to being excited as at a *ḥag*" (Oxf. Hebr. Lex.). More probably it is simply a derivative from *ḥag*, giddiness as a result of going round at the festival dance; it is used in Isa. xix. 17 in a metaphorical way.

p. 108). In Hos. xi. 4 the two words are used as parallels.
So that the reference in the psalm may well be to strings
of worshippers being called upon to join in the sacred
dance. Briggs' objection to an explanation of this kind
on the ground that this usage of *ḥag* is rare and early,
"not to be thought of in so late a psalm," is not valid
when one remembers the tenacity with which religious
customs and expressions are clung to. It is well to remember that this psalm belongs to the "Hallel" (Pss.
cxiii.–cxviii.), the most important of the festival psalms;
the "Hallel" was sung at all the great feasts. We shall
see presently that very clear evidence exists for the performance of the encircling of the altar during the singing
of this psalm in later days, as well as other dancing
during the great festivals. It may be taken for granted
that both kinds of dance were not innovations belonging
to subsequent ages, but the continuance of what had
been handed down for ages.

Further, one must take into consideration the idea
that underlies the ritual of the encirclement of a city,
such as we read of in Josh. vi., where the same root as
that for the ritual encompassing of the altar is used
(*sābab*). Through the whole account the religious element
in the undertaking comes strongly to the fore; the encircling procession is a sacred act: the sounding of the
rams' horns by the priests, seven in number, the presence
of the ark, the sevenfold encirclement on the seventh
day, all emphasize its religious character which receives
its highest stamp in the words which proclaim the
presence of Jahwe Himself in the procession: "And it
was so, that when Joshua had spoken unto the people, the
seven priests bearing the seven trumpets of rams' horns
before Jahwe passed on, and blew with the trumpets:

and the ark of the covenant of Jahwe followed them."
The God of the nation is conceived as being either
identified with, or present in, the ark. The meaning
and object of the encirclement is clear from the words
in vi. 17: "And the city shall be devoted, even it and
all that is therein, to Jahwe." It is, as it were, a magic
circle, described around the thing "devoted" in order
that nothing shall escape; by the encirclement it becomes "consecrated"; though, of course, in a different
sense from that in which the encirclement of the altar
consecrates the sacrifice on it.

Before drawing attention to some instances of this
type of dance among other peoples, mention may be
made of one among the Jews of post-biblical times. At
the Feast of Tabernacles, after the sacrifices had been
offered, the priests went in procession round the altar
singing Ps. cxviii. 25 on each of the seven days during
which the feast lasted. On the seventh day a sevenfold
circuit was made round the altar[1]. A ceremony of this
kind, as will be readily understood, would not have been
an innovation introduced in post-biblical times; we may
confidently take for granted that the usage, in one form
or another, had been handed down from time immemorial.

II

We have already drawn attention to the fact that the
central and most important part of the *cultus* of the
ancient Arabs was the circuit round the sanctuary, or,
when this was offered, round the sacrifice; and that it
was from this fact that the Ḥagg, which really means
the "sacred dance," got its name. This sacred dance

[1] Mishnah, *Sukkah*, iv. 2.

was performed not only round the *Kaaba*, but in every sanctuary round the sacred object. The holy stone is itself called *Davar*, "the object of encirclement," because of the custom of performing the sacred dance round it[1]. Another illustration of this type of sacred dance is given by Nilus. In speaking of the Arabs of the Sinaitic Peninsula, he says that they did not worship any god or image of a god, but sacrificed to the morning star at its rising. Then he goes on to describe how they took for their sacrifice a white camel which they forced into a kneeling posture and "went circling round it in a circuitous fashion," the reference being clearly to some form of processional dance, which is not, however, further described; but he mentions singing which went on at the same time, a very usual accompaniment to the sacred dance. When the third circuit had been made, and while the singing was still going on, the leader in the procession slaughtered the camel[2]. According to Jeremias this ritual perambulation (*ṭawâf*) round the altar or a sacrificial victim among the idolatrous Semites may be explained as having been a symbolic representation of the movement of the heavenly bodies, in which case, as he maintains, the ritual dance would be proved to be a product of the ancient oriental world-concept[3].

[1] See above, pp. 48 ff. The prince-poet Imra-al-Kais refers in one of his poems to girls, gown-clad, going swiftly round the *Davar* (*EB*, i. 998).

[2] *Nili Opera*, Narrat. iii. 8 (in Migne, *Patrol. Graec.* LXXIX. 612 f. "In later Arabia, the *ṭawâf*, or act of circling the sacred stone, was still a principal part of religion; but even before Mohammed's time it had begun to be dissociated from sacrifice, and became a meaningless ceremony," Robertson Smith, *op. cit.* p. 340.

[3] "Damit wäre dann der kultische Tanz als Produkt der altorientalischen Vorstellungswelt erwiesen" (de la Saussaye, *Religionsgeschichte*, i. 380 [1905]).

But the rite is susceptible of a different explanation as we have seen[1].

Another instructive example among the Semites, in which it is evident that the perambulation is not a symbolic representation of the movement of the heavenly bodies, is that which takes place at the festival of the Pyre at Heliopolis. Lucian describes this as follows:

The greatest of the festivals that they celebrate is that held in the opening of the spring; some call this the Pyre, others the Lamp. On this occasion the sacrifice is performed in this way. They cut down tall trees and set them up in the court; then they bring goats and sheep and cattle and hang them living to the trees; they add to these birds and garments, and gold and silver work. After all is finished, they carry the gods around the trees and set fire under; in a moment all is in a blaze. To this solemn rite a great multitude flocks from Syria and all the regions around. Each brings his own god and the statues which each has of his own gods[2].

This encircling procession of the gods will be referred to again when we review the instances of this type of sacred dance which have been gathered.

The suspending of the animals on trees reminds us—but the object is different—of the *Dhāt anwāt*, or "tree to hang things on"; the spirit of a departed saint is supposed to take up his abode in the tree at certain times, and his worshippers hang rags and ribbons on its branches as "pledges of attachment[3]"; this is still very common at the present day[4]. Dancing is, however, never

[1] See p. 94.
[2] *De Dea Syria*, XLIX.; see Strong and Garstang, *The Syrian Goddess*, and Garstang's notes on pp. 83 f. (1913).
[3] Robertson Smith, *op. cit.* pp. 185, 335.
[4] See Curtiss, *Primitive Semitic Religion To-day*, p. 91, where a good photograph of one of these trees is given.

mentioned in connexion with this.   But in the case of
the holy tree spoken of by the ancient Arabian historian,
Tabari, it is very probable that dancing was performed
round it, even though it is not specifically mentioned.
He tells of a lofty date-palm in Nĕgrān which the inhabitants worshipped, and in honour of which a festival
was celebrated annually; on these occasions they be-
decked the tree with as many beautiful women's garments
as could be procured, and during a whole day divine
honours were paid to it[1].

Once more, to take a modern example which may well
reflect traditional usage; among the Noṣairis, a Semitic
tribe inhabiting the mountainous country to the south
of the Orontes, and among whom many ancient customs
are preserved, a festival called the feast of St Barbe is
observed.   At this feast the young men and women,
after candles have been lighted, dance round the festival
board, which is covered with food of various kinds,
singing and shouting[2].   Apparently there is little religious significance in this now; but it is safe to say that
at some time of its history this dance constituted an act
of honour to the saint, or a predecessor.

We have been unable to find any further instances of
this type of sacred dance among Semitic peoples, nor
yet among the Egyptians.

III

Among the Greeks the dance round a sacred object
must have been very usual, judging from representations

[1] Nöldeke, *Geschichte der Perser und Araber zur Zeit der Sasani-
den*. Aus der arabischen Chronik des Tabari, p. 181 (1879). I am
indebted to the kindness of Prof. Bevan, of Cambridge, for this
reference.

[2] See Dussaud, *Histoire et Religion des Nosairis*, pp. 149 f.
(1900).

of it which have been found in Cyprus. Thus, a votive offering made of clay, found near the villages of Katy-data-Linu and now in the Cyprus Museum, is a very interesting example; it consists of three bearded men dancing round another, who is also bearded and who accompanies the dance on a Pan's-pipe. Aphrodite was the chief goddess worshipped in the locality. The workmanship is very rough and belongs, according to Ohnefalsch-Richter, to the 6th century B.C. One of the dancing figures is lost, but the three were originally clearly represented as dancing round the one in the centre with hands joined. "It shows a dance-group such as was so often formed at festivals of the gods by Aryans and Semites, Greeks and Hebrews[1]." Somewhat similar to this is another group (cxxxv. 6) of three women holding hands and dancing round another who is playing a Pan's-pipe. Another represents, as Ohnefalsch-Richter says, an Olympian dance (cxxxii. 3); in this case seven women are dancing round in a circle; the arms of each clasp the neighbour on either side round the waist. An example of the sexes dancing together is cxxxv. 6; this is of terra-cotta from Leukosia[2]; six figures are dancing in a semi-circle, two are playing the tympanum; they are alternately men and women (cp. the quotation from the *Iliad* given above: "Young men and comely damsels were dancing, that clasped each other by the wrist"). Again, a vessel of stone, which Ohnefalsch-Richter believes to have been a vessel for incense, forms a group of three women dancing in a circle with joined hands. It resembles many similar vessels found in the Artemis-

---

[1] Ohnefalsch-Richter, *op. cit.* i. 360; it is numbered xvii. 5 in vol. ii.

[2] Now in the Berlin Mus. Antiq., T.C. 668238.

Kybele *temenos* at Achna, in Cyprus, as well as in Artemis-Kybele groves; they are not found elsewhere; all represent three women, roughly formed in the "Egyptian style," and seem to have been a common cult-object in the worship of Artemis-Kybele[1]. Two examples representing a dance round a sacred tree may be mentioned. One is very roughly made of clay; three women holding hands are dancing round it (cxxxv. 4). In this case the representation is formed on a golden ring, from Mycenae; it is evidently intended to be a dance round a sacred tree. This kind of sacred dance, says Ohnefalsch-Richter, often occurs on Graeco-Phoenician bronze vases[2].

Finally, just a word may be said of the ceremony called the ἀμφιδρόμια, "the running round"; this was a purificatory rite for new-born infants[3]. The child was carried at a running pace round the domestic hearth, the idea being, presumably, that the proximity of the fire acted as a lustration; this does not, however, explain the running round for which there must have been some special reason; is it possible that the idea here was that the current of air, produced by the quick running round, which played upon the child, also had a purifying effect? Air was one of the means of lustration; the combination of fire and air would have afforded all that could be desired[4].

While this rite cannot be described as magical, it is not, strictly speaking, religious; it seems to be in a

---

[1] Ohnefalsch-Richter, *op. cit.* I. 360; numbered xvii. 6 in vol. II.
[2] *Op. cit.* I. 445; numbered cxxvii. 3 in vol. II.
[3] Cp. Suidas, s.v. 'Αμφιδρόμια.
[4] See Lobeck, *Aglao.*, 237 ff., 639 ff., 695 (1829); Bekker, *Anecdota Graeca*, p. 207 (1814–1821); Pauly, *Realencycl. der classischen Alterthumswissenschaft*, IV. 1240 ff. (1862).

sphere between the two; at the same time, judging from certain Roman rites to which we turn now, the ἀμφι-δρόμια at any rate approaches the border-line of religion.

IV

The type of sacred dance which we are considering does not seem to have been in vogue among the Romans excepting in the form of the circumambulatory procession; and although the word "dance" can only in an extended sense be applied to a procession, yet, as we have seen (pp. 5 f.), this is justified. The Romans worshipped their gods with sacrifice and prayer; the two, so far as is known, were invariably combined. But on important occasions, and for particular reasons, these were performed in the course of a procession or circuit round some object—land, city, army, or instruments, such as arms and trumpets—or, again, the whole Roman people, if supposed to be in need of 'purification' from some evil influence; in this extended form the ritual was called *lustratio*; and this ceremonial was perhaps the most characteristic, not only of the Roman, but of all ancient Italian forms of worship[1].

The object of this rite was, according to Wissowa[2], the purification of all that was within the circle formed by the procession; and as the sacred victims intended for sacrifice were taken round, the effect was to keep away all evil influences outside the circuit made.

A striking example of this circumambulatory procession was its performance by the *Fratres Arvales* at the festival of the *Ambarvalia*, to which reference is made below (p. 149). Another is that of the course of the

---

[1] Warde Fowler in *ERE*, x. 827 *b*.
[2] *Religion und Kultus der Römer*, p. 390 (1912).

Luperci round the Palatine Hill at the *Lupercalia* (see further, p. 150); this, too, had as its object purification whereby fruitfulness was imparted to the fruits of the field, and to the flocks.

As among the Greeks, so, too, the Romans had a purificatory rite for their new-born infants on the *dies lustricus, i.e.* on the ninth day after birth for boys, on the eighth for girls. Marquardt thinks that perhaps the Romans took over the rite from the Greeks[1].

V

Among uncultured races the sacred dance in a circle, or round some sacred object, is widely spread; many illustrations of it could be given, but it will suffice if quite a few examples are offered because, as there is a great family likeness between them, a few will answer the same purpose as a large number.

Schoolcraft tells us that among the Dakotahs a feast is held every now and then at which a special dance is performed in honour of their god Ha-o-Kah. He is a giant god, but subordinate to the Great Spirit. This dance

is performed by the men only, within a wigwam, around a fire over which are kettles of meat boiling. They have no clothing except a conical cap made of birch bark with paint to represent lightning, and some strips of the same material around the loins. While hopping and singing around the kettles they will thrust in their bare hands and pull out pieces of meat and eat them while scalding hot. After the meat is all eaten they will splash the hot water over their bare backs, all the time hopping around and singing out, "oh, how cold it is!" pretending that the hot water does not scald them, and that the god will not allow any of his clan to be injured by it.

[1] *Das Privatleben der Römer*, p. 83 and the notes (1886).

An illustration is given of the worshippers hopping round the fire[1].

Again, the Timagani Indians have a "Bear Dance" which is performed in the form of a circle led by the chief playing a drum and singing the "Bear Dance" song; the circle goes round counter-clockwise. The leader sometimes dances backwards, turns round, stoops, and in other ways imitates the bear....The circling keeps up until the song is finished. The idea of this dance seems to be to honour the bear by imitating him[2].

The performers in this dance do not encircle any object; it is simply a dance in the form of a circle; they do not hold hands, but go round in a follow-my-leader style. Although the dancing in honour of the bear reminds one of the Ἀρκτεία performed in honour of Artemis, it differs from this in that only men take part in it; and the Ἀρκτεία, in which the performers are only young girls is, as we have seen, an initiation ceremony. A closer parallel of the dance of the Timagani Indians is the "Bear Dance" among the Sioux Indians mentioned by Réville[3].

At the New Year festival of the Kayans of Sarāwak, to come to another part of the world, there is a great sacrifice of pigs, whose "spiritual essence is appropriately offered to the spirits, while their material substance is consumed by the worshippers."

"In carrying out this highly satisfactory arrangement," says Frazer, "while the live pigs lay tethered in a row on the ground, the priestesses dance solemnly round a sacrificial stage, each of them arrayed in a war-

[1] *The Indian Tribes of the United States*, I. 146 ff.; ed. by F. S. Drake (1891).
[2] Speck, *Ethnology of the Yuchi Indians*, p. 28 (1909).
[3] *Les Religions des Peuples Non-civilisés*, I. 269 (1883).

mantle of panther skin, and wearing a war-cap on her
head, and on either side two priests armed with swords
execute war-dances for the purpose of scaring away evil
spirits...[1]."

This encirclement of the sacrificial victims seems to be
a kind of consecrating act prior to the sacrifice similar
to the rite of the heathen Arabs in encircling their white
camel destined for sacrifice to the morning star. The
same is probably the case among the Bagobos of Min-
danao, one of the Philippine islands, who

perform a sacred dance round a human victim prior to
his sacrifice, offered for the purpose of making the crops
grow[2].

But the more usual rite for making the crops grow is
the sacred dance round a tree; the propitiation of the
tree-spirit is believed to be a potent means for securing
this end[3]. Thus the Gallas dance in couples round sacred
trees, praying for a good harvest. Every couple consists
of a man and a woman, who are linked together by a
stick, of which each holds one end. Under their arms
they carry green corn or grass[4]. This is the underlying
idea of the dances of a quasi-religious character round
the May-pole, and round the "Corn-Mother[5]," of which
there are such numberless instances. It is also supposed
to make the cattle thrive; one instance of numbers may
be given; the Wends used to attach an iron cock to an
oak; they danced round this and then drove their cattle

---

[1] GB, Spirits of the Corn..., I. 97.
[2] Frazer, GB, Spirits of the Corn..., I. 240 ff., II. 326 ff.; The
Scapegoat, 232 ff., 251 ff., 315.
[3] Mannhardt, Baumkultus, pp. 190 ff. (1875–1877); Wald- und
Feldkulte, I. 244 (1904–1905).
[4] Frazer, GB, The Magic Art, II. 47 ff.; see also the instances
mentioned above, p. 98.
[5] Frazer, GB, Spirits of the Corn..., I. 136 ff.

round it in the belief that by this means their cattle would increase[1].

We refrain from offering further examples, for everyone knows how common this custom was, and still is.

* * * *

SUMMARY AND CONSIDERATIONS

The objects around which dances were performed were various. In the Old Testament dancing is not mentioned around trees and wells, but as these were often sacred and as, in consequence, the dance around them was very common among many peoples, it is a reasonable assumption that the Israelites did the same. The song to the well in Num. xxi. 17, 18 strengthens this assumption, especially in view of the two parallels given. The definite mention of dancing in connexion with the Golden Calf (it is not specifically stated that the dancing was *round* it, but this would have been the most obvious form for it to take) suggests the probability that similar idols in other sanctuaries were similarly honoured.

The ceremonial encirclement of the altar, whatever the form of the encircling procession, is sufficiently attested in the Old Testament, though the text is uncertain in three of the passages cited. The usage in later days among the Jews must be regarded as the continuance of ancient custom. The analogy of the encirclement of a city is appropriate in this connexion. The object of the encircling procession round a city seems to be that of "devoting" all that is within it, which thereby becomes *taboo*. The encirclement of the altar is an act of consecration, *i.e.* of the sacrifice upon it. This explanation of the rite is suggested by the analogous

[1] Mannhardt, *Baumkultus*, p. 174; Frazer, *The Magic Art*, II. 58 ff.

custom among the Arabs of encircling a sacrificial victim. The contention that the encircling procession was a symbolic representation of the movement of the heavenly bodies does not explain why it should take place round a *sacrificial victim*. The rite seems more likely to have had the object of consecration; and this receives confirmation from the instance recorded by Lucian among the Syrians who perambulated their gods round the sacrificial victims; this can scarcely have had any other meaning than that of sanctifying all within the divine circle traced by the gods.

The dance round a sacred object must have been very common among the Greeks, judging by the large number of representations of it which have come down to us; the Cyprus "finds" are full of interest. Those which represent the dance round a person who accompanies it on a Pan's-pipe probably portrays the kind of dancing which took place at festivals when numbers of such groups were formed. Such dances must often have degenerated into mere "fun"; but that they originally had a serious side and were performed with the single purpose of doing something pleasing in the sight of a god or goddess, does not admit of doubt. The representations may well reflect one form of dancing at Israelite festivals. Among the Greeks we have direct evidence of these "ring" dances being performed by men and women together; and it is known that this led at times to unseemly licence. What little evidence we have on the subject so far as the Israelites were concerned points to the fact that the sexes danced separately; whether this was always so must be left undetermined. The examples of the dance round the sacred tree are instructive; it was undoubtedly practised by all peoples among whom trees were objects of worship, and therefore in all probability among the Israelites. The ἀμφιδρόμια, or purificatory rite of running round new-born infants, practised by the Greeks and Romans, had no parallel among the Israelites, so far as we know. But the ritual *lustratio* of the Romans may well throw light on the Israelite ritual of encircling the altar, referred to above.

The dance of the Dakotahs round the flesh-pot was performed purely in honour of the god; it partakes in some sense of an act of faith, for the believers persuade themselves that their god will not permit his worshippers to be scalded by the boiling water; whether their faith ever reached the height of neutralizing sensation is not recorded. The Bear Dance of the Timagani Indians and of the Sioux North American Indians must have a point of attachment somewhere with the Ἀρκτεία danced in honour of Artemis. The dance of the Kayans, as well as the Bagobos, around sacrificial victims appears to serve a consecrating purpose.

One of the original objects of the dance round the sacred tree is seen from the practice among the Gallas to be to make the crops grow; the tree-spirit who looks after these things is propitiated by the dance in his honour. It is difficult to resist the surmise that at one time the Israelites did the same thing. Tree-spirits, it is true, have not necessarily anything to do with the crops, and we may be certain that in many cases there was no connexion between sacred trees and the growth of the crops among the Israelites; but they were an agricultural people, and the belief in the influence of tree-spirits upon the growth of the crops is so widespread that the probability of its existence among the Israelites must be reckoned with.

CHAPTER VII

THE ECSTATIC DANCE

I

An important department of our subject is that of the type of dance performed by the early prophets of Israel. We say the "early" prophets because the one account which the Old Testament gives us of this kind of dance refers to it among the early prophets. There is, however, no reason for supposing—rather the contrary[1]—that this type of the sacred dance was confined to the *early* prophets of Israel. Its purpose was connected with an aspiration deeply seated in human nature; its performance has been very widespread among peoples of antiquity; and it is found to exist at the present day among uncultured races. So that the presumption is that it did not cease abruptly among the Israelites, but continued, at any rate, up to the time of the Exile.

This type of dance is the outcome of strong religious emotion which necessitates some bodily expression. It may be paralleled with the exuberance of physical health which demands vigorous exercise. While it begins with moderated movements, held in check by rhythmical restraint, yet as the nervous excitement of the performer becomes increasingly intense and the physical exertion more exacting, so does the dance get wilder and wilder until, as the result of the abandonment of all self-control, the dancer ultimately loses conscious-

[1] On the subject generally see Hölscher, *Die Profeten: Untersuchungen zur Religionsgeschichte Israels*, pp. 129–158 (1914).

ness. Its contagious character has often been remarked upon.

But the religious emotion which thus finds expression is engendered by an aspiration which is believed to be attained by means of the dance; and this aspiration is nothing less than union with the deity. The loss of consciousness which eventually takes place is replaced, so it is believed, by the indwelling of the divine spirit; the body thus becomes the temporary abode of the deity, and is utilized for divine purposes.

The first passage in the Old Testament with which we are specially concerned is 1 Sam. x. 5 ff.:

...and it shall come to pass, when thou art come thither to the city, that thou shalt meet a band (*ḥebel*) of prophets coming down from the high place (*bāmāh*), and in front of them harp and drum and pipe and lyre, and they shall be prophesying...,

cp. xix. 20–24. It is true, no direct mention of the sacred dance is made here, but in view of the enumeration of musical instruments which, as we have seen, usually accompanied dancing, it is reasonable to assume that a ritual dance was taking place. That it was a religious exercise of some kind is made clear by the fact that they had come down from the high place (*bāmāh*), *i.e.* a sanctuary. The technical name for such a band of prophets, *ḥebel*, "rope" or "string" (cp. Josh. ii. 15), shows that the procession was in single file[1]; with which we may com-

---

[1] In speaking of the exercises of the early prophetical bands Robertson Smith says that "they were sometimes gone through in sacred processions, sometimes at a fixed place, as at the Naioth at Ramah, which ought probably to be rendered 'dwellings'—a sort of coenobium. They were accompanied by music of a somewhat noisy character, in which the hand-drum and the pipe played a part, as was otherwise the case in festal processions to the sanctuary (2 Sam. vi. 5; Isa. xxx. 29). Thus the religious exercises of the prophets seem to be a development in a peculiar direction of

pare the sacred dance in single file depicted on the Hittite inscription at Boghazkeui (see p. 59). The account given in the Old Testament of the "prophesying" of these early prophets, and of the means employed whereby they reached the pitch of excitement required for the purpose, is so sober and restrained that it would be difficult to form a picture of the whole proceeding without the help of analogous performances among other peoples. And we are justified in believing that the practice of this type of dance among other peoples does throw light on its mode of performance among these Israelite prophets, because it is a question here of a phenomenon, a curious phenomenon, which appears at a certain stage of religious development, with few exceptions, all over the world. Its details may, and do, differ; but the essence of the rite is the same. There are innate tendencies in human nature which produce similar results; and this is one of them. So that when the means used for producing such results are given in greater detail in many cases, we are justified in believing them to have been similar in a case in which, for some reason or other, the details are only partially described. But if the details of the means used to produce the result are somewhat lacking in the Old Testament account, the result itself is stated clearly enough. The object of all that took place was to be "possessed,"—in this case by the spirit of Jahwe; for it was this "possession," this indwelling of the deity, which enforced the "prophesying." In the passage before us the centre of interest, in the eyes of

the ordinary forms of Hebrew worship at the time, and the fact that the 'prophesying' was contagious establishes its analogy to other contagious forms of religious excitement" (*The Prophets of Israel*, p. 392 [1897]). See further, Gressmann, *Palestinas Erdgeruch in der Israelitischen Religion*, pp. 34 ff. (1909).

the writer, is Saul. Of him it is said that, as a result of his contact with the "rope" of prophets prophesying, "the spirit of Jahwe" would come "mightily" upon him, and that he, too, would prophesy with them, and "be turned into another man"; the context shows that his contact with the prophets meant joining in their ecstatic dance, the effect of which is graphically described in verses 11, 12:

And it came to pass, when all that knew him beforetime saw that, behold, he prophesied with the prophets, then the people said one to another, What is this that is come unto the son of Kish? Is Saul also among the prophets?...

The surprise here expressed was natural enough seeing the extravagances to which the ecstatic state led, for in xix. 24 it is said of Saul that as one of the results of his "possession" he "stripped off his clothes...and lay down naked all that day and all that night."

The point with which we are primarily concerned is the means employed to get oneself into the ecstatic state required in order to become "possessed." As is well known, these were of various kinds; but the one most prevalent in antiquity, as well as among men in a low stage of culture at the present day, was, and is, the sacred dance accompanied by music. While there is only one other passage (on which see below) in the Old Testament which deals in any detail with this type of sacred dance, it would be the greatest mistake to suppose that it was of only rare occurrence[1]. In the passage just referred to, there is no hint as to its being anything unusual; the only thing unusual was Saul's "possession," while the very saying, "Is Saul also among the prophets?" points to the peculiarity of the prophets as something recognized and well known. And from what

[1] Robertson Smith, *The Religion of the Semites*, p. 432.

we gather as to the existence of the ecstatic dance among other peoples, the fact of its existence among the Israelites does not strike one as other than what one would expect.

But we turn now to another passage in which we read of a sacred dance of a peculiar kind which seems to develop into an orgiastic form of ecstatic dance. This was a ritual limping dance performed at sanctuaries, and apparently in cases of great emergency. Its object was not the same as that form of it to which we have just referred; however, as it evidently must belong to the category of ecstatic dances, we consider it here. The passage is the familiar one, 1 Kings xviii. 26, where it is said that the prophets of Baal executed a special kind of limping dance around the altar: "They limped about the altar which was made." This was done after the ineffectual calling upon the name of their god from morning till noon, so that it seems to have been regarded by them as a special means of appeal to which recourse was had as a last resort. The dance consisted of a step which had the effect of making the dancers look lame[1]. This is clear from the use of the root in other connexions. Thus, Mephibosheth "became lame" (2 Sam. iv. 4 and ix. 13), as the result of a fall. The same root is used in reference to men who are lame in 2 Sam. v. 6–8, and also in Lev. xxi. 18, where a lame man is not permitted "to offer bread to his God." It is also used in reference to animals not regarded as fit to be sacrificed because of lameness (Deut. xv. 21, Mal. i. 8–13; cp. also Isa. xxxiii. 23, xxxv. 6, Jer. xxxi. 8, Prov. xxvi. 7, Job xxix. 15; and as a proper name it occurs in 1 Chron. iv. 12, Ezra ii. 49, Neh. iii. 6, vii. 51). In a figurative way,

[1] See, for interesting parallels, S. A. Cook, in *Essays and Studies presented to William Ridgeway*, p. 397 (1913).

but connoting the same idea, the word occurs in 1 Kings
xviii. 21: "How long will ye limp upon two legs?" That
the prophet is making a word-play here is obvious; but
the passage raises the question as to the kind of step in
which the dance was performed. Limping on two legs
can hardly mean that the "limping" was done on both
legs at the same time, for a frog-leap of this kind would
not suggest lameness! The limp must have been done
on either leg alternately, yet neither leg being raised
from the ground; as this involves the bending of the
knees, one can form a fairly clear idea of what this dance
looked like. The word for "legs" is used in Isa. xvii. 6,
xxvii. 10 of the forked branches of a tree, cp. Ezek. xxxi.
6–8; if one pictures to oneself such a fork, gnarled and
bent, it might certainly suggest the position of a man's
legs while performing this dance. The purpose of this
curious dance-step may well have been that by simu-
lating lameness it was thought that the pity of the god
would be aroused, and that he would therefore be moved
to answer petitions. As Robertson Smith says, "the
limping dance of the priests of Baal in 1 Kings xviii. 26
is associated with forms of mournful supplication, and
in Syriac the same verb, in different conjugations, means
'to dance' and 'to mourn[1].'" While the dance began in
sober style[2] it gradually increased to an orgiastic frenzy,
as is clear from verse 28: "And they cried aloud, and cut
themselves after their manner with knives and lances,
till the blood gushed out upon them"; cp. Hos. vii. 14[3].

[1] *The Religion of the Semites*, p. 432. But see S. A. Cook in the
work just cited.
[2] The R.V. rendering of 1 Kings xviii. 26, "And they leaped
about the altar," is misleading.
[3] The text emendation here is obvious, it should be *yithgôdâdu*
("they cut themselves") for *yithgôrâru* ("they assemble themselves").

This dance was performed by the prophets of Baal, and it may therefore be objected that it does not reflect Israelite usage because the worship of these prophets was Phoenician (cp. 1 Kings xvi. 30–33); but to this it must be replied that the Old Testament gives ample evidence to show that the influence of the indigenous cults of the land was very powerful upon the Israelites[1]; the prophet Elijah himself regards practically the whole nation as under this influence (1 Kings xix. 10, 18). Moreover, we have mention of a ritual dance similar to that just referred to in Gen. xxxii. 30, 31 (31, 32 in Hebr.), though the word used is a different one (*zala‘*):

And Jacob called the name of the place Peniel; for I have seen God face to face, and my life is preserved. And the sun rose upon him as he passed over Penuel, and he limped upon his thigh.

We must see here, as Gunkel points out, an aetiological *trait*: "Just as, and because, Jacob limped in Penuel, so are we also wont to limp in Penuel[2]." The name implies that it was a sanctuary, a name such as "the face of God" proves that here a god was believed to manifest himself[3]; and, whatever may have originally been the reason for it, it was the custom at this sanctuary to perform the "limping" dance. It took place at sunrise (see verse 31), so that it may at one time have had something to do with sun-worship.

Conceivably another ancient sanctuary where this

---

[1] This has been illustrated by the excavations on the site of ancient Gezer undertaken by the Palestine Exploration Fund.

[2] *Genesis*, p. 329 (1901).

[3] See, further, von Gall, *Altisraelitische Kultstätten*, pp. 148 ff. (1898).

special kind of dance was performed was *Zēla*ʿ[1], the name of Saul's ancestral dwelling-place (2 Sam. xxi. 14).

Although the passages in the Old Testament in which this type of sacred dance is referred to are not numerous, they are sufficient to show that the ecstatic dance was not unknown among the Israelites. We have already shown reasons to account for the comparative paucity of references in the Old Testament to the religious dance generally; what we have said applies to this limping dance with special force, since there are grounds for believing it to have been of Syrian origin; as characteristic of Syrian religion it would have been regarded with special abhorrence by Israelite religious leaders as being the heathen rite of that form of alien cult to the influence of which the Israelites were most exposed.

It will have been noticed that mention has been made of what are, in effect, two distinct forms of what for the want of a better term we have called the ecstatic dance, viz. that which had for its object the bringing about of a state of semi-consciousness, or total unconsciousness, during which state the deity was believed to take up his abode in the body of the worshipper, *i.e.* union with the deity; and that which had for its purpose the enforcing of the deity to answer prayer. They differed in important particulars, to which we shall refer again; but that wherein they were similar was the state of wild frenzy which both ultimately assumed.

[1] The word is also used for limping, or stumbling, in a figurative sense (Jer. xx. 10 and elsewhere; in Job xviii. 12, Ball would read *balaʿ*). According to Driver the cognate Arabic word means "to curve" (*Oxford Hebr. Lex.*); one thinks of the bent or curved position of the body during the performance of the "limping" dance.

We shall now draw attention to some examples of both forms of this ecstatic dance among other peoples.

II

It is a significant fact that, with the exception of Syria, there is scarcely any evidence of the existence of the ecstatic dance among the Semites. In the great mass of Babylonian and Assyrian texts of which translations have been published[1] many refer to ritual of various kinds; in these some incidental references to this type of dance might have been expected to occur had such been in existence. We have sought in vain among many of these translated texts for any hint of it; nor have we been able to find in the works of authoritative writers on Assyro-Babylonian religion any allusion to it. It may, we believe, be accepted as a fact that the ecstatic dance was unknown among these people; and this would accord with what is otherwise known of their religious practices, which were austere and restrained.

What has been said applies also to the ancient Egyptians; evidence for the existence of this type of religious dance does not appear on the inscriptions, nor yet in Egyptian texts[2]. On the other hand, one has only to think of the Dancing Dervishes to realize that the ecstatic dance exists in Egypt at the present day. Tristram compares the dancing of the modern dervishes with that of the early Israelite prophets; and he gives an interesting description of Arabi Pasha leading a procession with the sacred carpet for the Kaaba of Mecca

[1] See the various works of Schrader, Winckler, Zimmern, Jensen, O. Weber, Jastrow, etc.

[2] See, e.g., Wiedemann, *Die Religion der alten Aegypter*, pp. 85–87 (1890); Erman, *Die ägyptische Religion*, pp. 61 f., 90 (1909), and the works of other authorities mentioned in previous chapters.

out of Cairo on its way to the Prophet's shrine; "in front," he says, "was a vast crowd of ulemas and dervishes, leaping, bounding, swaying their arms, and whirling round in time to the din of drums, trumpets, and cymbals which followed them[1]." One feels that there must be a long history behind this, and though the evidence is wanting it is difficult to believe that there was not something of the kind in ages long since past.

Again, as to the ancient Arabs, there is almost as great a dearth of evidence, though some slight indications exist of this type of dance having been performed in days gone by[2]. Thus, a proceeding very similar to that of Saul is mentioned by Robertson Smith of Kûkubûry, who used "under the influence of religious music, to become so excited as to pull off part of his clothes"; like Saul he was what the Arabs would now call *malbûs*[3]. This type of dance exists at the present day among the Arabs, and it is interesting to note, among other things, that it is regarded as a means to mystic experiences[4].

Fuller information is forthcoming with regard to the ancient Syrians.

There is the interesting story of Wen-Amon, an Egyptian official who came to Byblos in Phoenicia in the 11th century B.C. Here we are told of how a noble youth, while he was sacrificing to his gods, was seized by the

---

[1] *Eastern Customs in Bible Lands*, pp. 207–210 (1894); a good account of the Dancing Dervishes is given in W. Tyndale's *An Artist in Egypt*, pp. 26–30 (1912); and see especially Gressmann, *Palestinas Erdgeruch in der Israelitischen Religion*, pp. 34 ff. (1909).

[2] See Herodotus, II. 133.

[3] *The Prophets of Israel*, p. 392 (1897); cp. Stade, *Geschichte des Volkes Israel*, I. 477 (1886).

[4] Snouck-Hurgronje, *Mekka*, II. 281 (1888–1889). And see, further, Doughty, *Arabia Deserta*, II. 119 (orig. ed.); Robinson Lees mentions this dancing as taking place at holy places in Palestine, *Village Life in Palestine*, pp. 27, 28 (1897).

god who caused him to fall into a state of ecstasy; the hieroglyph depicts a man rushing forward with outstretched arms. While the youth is in this state he prophesies, declaring that a certain messenger who had arrived had indeed brought the image of a god, and must be received, for he had been sent by Amon. This occurs as the messenger with his god is on the point of being sent away. We are not concerned with the various details of this story; the point is that a youth is supposed to have been caused by the will of the god to fall into an ecstasy; the hieroglyph clearly implies an ecstatic dance; and as a result he reveals the arrival of another god brought by the messenger. He speaks while in this state of ecstasy words which are divinely put into his mouth, so that he is the mouthpiece of the god[1]. This is precisely the same idea as that of the spirit of Jahwe coming mightily upon Saul, he prophesies, and is turned into another man.

Another example is given by Heliodorus (*Aethiopica*, iv. 16 f.), who describes the sacred dance of the Tyrian seafarers in the worship of the Tyrian Herakles; he says:

And I left them there with their flutes and their dances, which they performed after the manner of the Assyrians [*i.e.* Syrians], hopping to the accompaniment of the quick music of the Pektides, now jumping up with light leaps, now limping along on the ground, and then turning with the whole body, spinning around like men possessed[2].

[1] See Golénischeff, *Recueil de Travaux*, xxi. 22 f.; Gressmann, *Altorientalische Texte und Bilder zum A.T.*, i. 225 ff. (1909).

[2] Regarding the musical accompaniment to such ecstatic dances, Iamblichus propounds the extraordinary theory that the reason why certain sounds and melodies produce an ecstatic state is because before the soul entered the body it was "an auditor of divine harmony," and when, being in the body, it hears these, it recollects the divine harmony and participates in it; hence the cause of the ecstatic state and the faculty of divination (*De Mysteriis*, iii. 9 end).

The limping here recalls the dance of the prophets of Baal, or rather of its earlier phase, and that of Jacob at Penuel. For the wilder phase of the dance of these prophets we have a very interesting parallel given by Apuleius of the ecstatic dance of the priests of the Syrian goddess. This is well worth giving in full; it occurs in *The Golden Ass*, VIII. 27, 28:

The day following I saw them apparelled in divers colours, and hideously tricked out, having their faces ruddled with paint, and their eyes tricked out with grease, mitres on their heads, vestments coloured like saffron, surplices of silk and linen; and some ware white tunics painted with purple stripes which pointed every way like spears, girt with belts, and on their feet were yellow shoes. And they attired the goddess in silken robe, and put her upon my back. Then they went forth with their arms naked to their shoulders, bearing with them great swords and mighty axes, shouting and dancing, like mad persons, to the sound of the pipe. After that we had passed many small villages, we fortuned to come to a certain rich man's house, where, at our first entry, they began to howl all out of tune and hurl themselves hither and thither as though they were mad. They made a thousand gests with their feet and their heads; they would bend down their necks, and spin round so that their hair flew out at a circle; they would bite their own flesh; finally, everyone took his two-edged weapon and wounded his arms in divers places. Meanwhile, there was one more mad than the rest, that fetched many deep sighs from the bottom of his heart, as though he had been ravished in spirit, or replenished with divine power, and he feigned a swoon and frenzy, as if (forsooth) the presence of the gods were not wont to make men better than before, but weak and sickly....And therewithal he took a whip, such as is naturally borne by these womanish men, with many twisted knots and tassels of wool, and strung with sheep's knuckle-bones, and with the knotted thongs scourged his own body, very strong to bear the pain of the blows, so that you might see the ground to be wet and defiled with the womanish blood that issued out abundantly with the cutting of the swords and the blows of the scourge...[1].

The close parallel of this procedure of these Syrian priests with that of the prophets of Baal needs no insisting upon.

III

We turn now to Greek sources; and here the material is as abundant as it is interesting; the examples to be given are therefore restricted in number, but they will be sufficient to illustrate the important part that this type of dance played in Greek religious ritual.

[1] Die sequenti variis coloribus indusiati et deformiter quisque formati, facie caenoso pigmento delita et oculis obunctis graphice prodeunt, mitellis et crocotis et carbasinis et bambycinis iniecti, quidam tunicas albas in modum lanciolarum quoquoversum fluente purpura depictas cingulo subligati, pedes luteis induti calceis; deamque serico contectam amiculo mihi gerendam imponunt brachiisque suis humero tenus renundatis, attollentes immanes gladios ac secures, evantes exsiliunt incitante tibiae cantu lymphaticum tripudium. Nec paucis pererratis casulis ad quandam villam possessoris beati perveniunt et ab ingressu primo statim absonis ululatibus constrepentes fanatice pervolant, diuque capite demisso cervices lubricis intorquentes motibus crinesque pendulos in circulum rotantes, et nonnunquam morsibus suos incursantes musculos, ad postremum ancipiti ferro quod gerebant sua quisque brachia dissicant. Inter haec unus ex illis bacchatur effusius ac de imis praecordiis anhelitus crebros referens, velut numinis divino spiritu repletus, simulabat sauciam vecordiam, prorus quasi deum praesentia soleant homines non sui fieri meliores sed debiles effici vel aegroti....Arrepto denique flagro, quod semiviris illis proprium gestamen est, contortis taeniis lanosi velleris prolixe fimbriatum et multiiugis talis ovium tesseratum, indidem sese multinodis commulcat ictibus, mire contra plagarum dolores praesumptione munitus. Cerneres prosectu gladiorum ictuque flagrorum solum spurcitia sanguinis effeminati madescere.... The translation is that of S. Gaselee in "Loeb Classical Library" (1915).

By way of introduction the following words of Farnell[1] will be found instructive; he is dealing with the earliest period of Greek religion, and in writing about the worship of Dionysos, says he was

vaguer in outline (than Apollo or Athene), a changeful power conceived more in accordance with daimonistic, later with pantheistic, thought, incarnate in many animal-shapes, and operative in the life-processes of the vegetative world; and an atmosphere of Nature-magic accompanied him;

then he goes on to say that

the central motives of this oldest form of ritual were the birth and death of the god—a conception pregnant of ideas that were to develop in the religious future, but alien to the ordinary Hellenic theology, though probably not unfamiliar to the earlier Cretan-Mycenaean creed. But the death of this god was partly a fact of ritual; he was torn to pieces by his mad worshippers and devoured sacramentally, for the bull or the goat or the boy that they rent and devoured was supposed to be his temporary incarnation, so that by this savage, and at times cannibalistic, communion they were filled with his blood and his spirit, and acquired miraculous powers. By such an act, and—we may suppose—by the occasional use of intoxicants and other nervous stimulants, the psychic condition that this worship evoked was frenzy and ecstasy, which might show itself in a wild outburst of mental and physical force, and which wrought up the enthusiastic feeling of self-abandonment, whereby the worshipper escaped the limits of his own nature and achieved a temporary sense of identity with the god, which might avail him even after death. This privilege of ecstasy might be used for the practical purposes of vegetation-magic, yet was desired and pro-

---

[1] In *ERE*, vi. 403 *a*; we give the quotation in full as this large Encyclopaedia is not, for many, easily accessible.

claimed for its own sake as a more intense mood of life. This religion preached no morality, and could ill adapt itself to civic life; its ideal was supernormal psychic energy. It is only one aspect of the ritual of this religion with which we are now concerned, and which is to be illustrated by the examples given, namely, the ecstatic dance which played such an important part in it. Therefore we naturally think of the mythic Maenads[1], and more especially of their historical counterpart, the Thyiads, who are much the same as the female Bacchantes. According to the myth concerning the origin of the Thyiads, they were so called because the first priestess of Dionysos was named Thyia, and she performed orgiastic dances in his honour; hence all women who danced, or "went mad," in honour of Dionysos were called Thyiads after her. The Maenads are depicted on many Greek vases and bas-reliefs, so that we can form a good idea of the kind of dances they were supposed to perform; and these were, of course, the actual form of the dances executed by the Thyiads. Thus, for example, on a vase in the Naples Museum four Maenads are represented dancing; two, with head thrown back, carry the thyrsus, a staff with vine-leaves, at the top of which was a pine-cone. One of them has also a torch; two others, while dancing, play, one a tambourine, the other a pipe[2]. Or again, on a cup in the Athens National Museum a Maenad is represented playing a tambourine, or timbrel, and dancing in wild fashion[3]. Another ex-

[1] On the Korybantes, the mythical attendants on Kybele, who were supposed to dance in wild fashion with the goddess on the mountains, see Rohde, *Psyche...*, II. 48 ff. (1907); the name was also given to the eunuch priests of the goddess in Phrygia.

[2] Panofka, *Dionysos und Thyiden*, pl. I. 2 (1853).

[3] Harrison, *Prolegomena to the Study of Greek Religion*, p. 453 (1903).

ample is the dancing, accompanied by instrumental
music, which is portrayed on the beautiful cylix of
Hieron, "perhaps the most exquisite that ceramography
has left us[1]"; the movements of the maidens are
superbly executed. But instances of this kind could be
greatly multiplied; they all exhibit one or other phase
of orgiastic dance, "the same mad revelry, the utter
exhaustion and prostrate sleep[2]"; and they represent
the kind of dancing which historically was performed by
the Thyiads. "Maenad," as Miss Harrison says, "is the
Mad One, Thyiad the Rushing Distraught One, or something of the kind...Mad One, Distraught One, Pure One,
are simply ways of describing a woman under the influence of a god, of Dionysos[3]"; and, of course, this
madness could be caused by any other orgiastic divinity.

Those who took part in these dances are described as
"raving and possessed"; their over-wrought state caused
them to see visions[4]; the god was believed to be present,
though invisible; and at the Dionysos festivals the
maidens celebrated his presence[5], thus direct contact
with him by his worshippers was effected[6].

In an interesting passage in Pausanias we read:

But I could not understand why he (i.e. Homer, in
Od. xi. 581) spoke of the fair dancing grounds of
Panopeus till it was explained to me by the women
whom the Athenians call Thyiades. The Thyiads are

[1] The treasure is in the Berlin Museum, Cat. 2290; Harrison,
op. cit., p. 428.
[2] Harrison, op. cit. p. 393; see also Gruppe, Griechische Mythologie und Religionsgeschichte, i. 162, ii. 840, 1293; Lobeck, Aglao.,
ii. 1085 ff.; Bekker, Anecdota Graeca, i. 234.
[3] Harrison, op. cit. p. 397; Gruppe, op. cit. ii. 748, 1293;
Reinach, Orpheus, p. 123.
[4] Philo, De Vita Contempl. ii.   [5] Diodorus, iv. iii. 2.
[6] Rohde, Psyche, ii. 11 ff.; Roscher, Ausführliches Lexikon...,
ii. 2243–2283 (1894–1897).

Attic women who go every other year with the Delphian
women to Parnassos, and there hold orgies in honour of
Dionysos. It is the custom of these Thyiads to dance
at various places on the road from Athens, and one of
these places is Panopeus. Thus, the epithet which
Homer applies to Panopeus seems to allude to the dance
of the Thyiads[1].

The finest and most graphic description of this ecstatic
dance is that given by Aristophanes in the *Frogs*,
325 ff. which is sung by the chorus of the Mystae:

> Thou that dwellest in the shadow
> Of great glory here beside us,
> Spirit, Spirit, we have hied us
> To thy dancing in the meadow!
> Come, Iacchus; let thy brow
> Toss its fruited myrtle bough;
> We are thine, O happy dancer; O our comrade, come
> and guide us!
> Let the mystic measure beat:
> Come in riot fiery feet;
> Free and holy all before thee,
> And thy Mystae wait the music of thy feet!
>
> Spirit, Spirit, lift the shaken
> Splendour of thy tossing torches!
> All the meadow flashes, scorches:
> Up, Iacchus, and awaken!
> Come, thou star that bringest light
> To the darkness of our rite,
> Till thine old men dance as young men, dance with every
> thought forsaken.
> Of the dulness and the fear
> Left by many a circling year:
> Let thy red light guide the dances
> Where thy banded youth advances,
> To be joyous by the blossoms of the mere![2]

[1] Pausan. x. iv. 1, 2.
[2] Harrison, *op. cit.* p. 540 (omitting the interjected words of
Xanthias and Dionysos).

Iacchus was the name by which Dionysos was known at Eleusis[1].

Pindar, in the Pythian Ode, refers to the dancing of the Thyiads at the annual festival celebrated in honour of Pan, when, according to Herodotus, vi. 105, sacrifice was offered and a torch procession took place:

I would pray to the Mother to loose her ban,
The holy goddess to whom, and to Pan,
Before my gate, all night long,
The maids do worship with dance and song[2].

Reference may also be made to Pausanias, v. xvi. 5, where we read of the "Sixteen Women" who get up two choruses, that of Physcoa and that of Hippodamia; the former was loved by Dionysos, and she is said to have been the first to pay reverence to him; and therefore "among the honours which Physcoa receives is a chorus named after her and arranged by the Sixteen Women."

The Thyiads are, as already mentioned, the same as the female Bacchantes often spoken of. Pausanias, for example, makes a reference to them:

...Beyond the theatre is a temple of Dionysos; the image of the god is of gold and ivory, and beside it are female Bacchantes in white marble. They say that these women are sacred, and that they rave in honour of Dionysos[3].

It is to these that Euripides refers in the Bacchae[4]. Diodorus speaks of them thus:

...In many towns of Greece every alternate year Bacchanalian assemblies of women gather together, and

[1] See Mommsen, op. cit. p. 224; cp. Foucart, Les grands mystères d'Eleusis, pp. 121 f.; and for the dancing at the celebration of the mysteries, see p. 142 (1904).
[2] Quoted by Harrison, Pyth. iii. 77.
[3] Pausan. ii. vii. 6. Cp. also Lobeck, Aglao., ii. 1088; Reinach, Orpheus, pp. 153 ff.
[4] Lines 680–691.

it is the custom for maidens to carry the thyrsus and to revel together, honouring and glorifying the god; and for the (married) women to worship the god in organized bands, and to revel in every way to celebrate the presence of Dionysos, imitating thereby the Maenads who from of old, it is said, constantly attended the god[1].

The male correlatives of Maenads, or rather Thyiads, are the Kouretes, who took their part in the Orphic mysteries. They were

the young population considered as worshipping the young male god, the Kouros; they were "mailed priests" because the young male population were naturally warriors. They danced their local war-dance over the new-born child, and, because in those early days the worship of the Mother and the son was not yet sundered, they were attendants (*prospoloi*) on the Mother also... they are divine (*theoi*), and their dancing is sacred[2].

Clement of Alexandria refers to them thus:

The mysteries of Dionysos are wholly inhuman; for while he was still a child and the Kouretes were dancing their armed dance about him, the Titans stole upon him, deceived him with childish toys, and tore him to pieces[3].

A typical instance of myth regarded as reality. We are only dealing here, however, with a *few* examples of the ecstatic dance among the Greeks. Those given will suffice for present purposes.

[1] iv. 3.

[2] Harrison, *op. cit.* p. 500; and the same author's *Themis*, pp. 23 ff. (1912). Rohde, *Psyche*, I. 272.

[3] *Protr.* II. 12. Concerning them Gruppe says: "Die Kureten, nach denen ein Magistratskollegium hiess, das unter dem *proto-koures* mystische Opfer feierte, sollten durch den Lärm der Waffen Hera vertrieben haben; eine Sagenbildung, die auf eine Angleichung an die Riten die zwar ebenfalls euboisch-boiotischen, aber vielleicht erst hier mit dem Artemis-dienst in Verbindung gesetzten Kultus der grossen Göttin hinweist" (*Griech. Myth.* I. 284; see also II. 820, 898, 1106, 1198).

It will have been noticed that all these examples present the ecstatic dance in its milder form; it is comparable with the dance of the Israelite prophets, not with that of the Syrian prophets of Baal. The fact is that this latter form of worship was not popular among the Greeks. It is true, the worship of Attis, in which the ecstatic dance in its most barbaric form figured prominently, is mentioned in Pausan. VII. xvii. 9, xx. 3; but this is quite exceptional, for the rites, of Syrian origin, which were performed in honour of Kybele and Attis were un-Hellenic and did not appeal to the Greeks.

"The barbarous and cruel character of the worship, with its frantic excesses, was doubtless repugnant to the good taste and humanity of the Greeks, who seem to have preferred the kindred but gentler rites of Adonis. Yet," continues the same writer, "the same features which shocked and repelled the Greeks may have positively attracted the less refined Romans and barbarians of the West. The ecstatic frenzies, which were mistaken for divine inspiration, the mangling of the body, the theory of a new birth, and the remission of sins through the shedding of blood, have all their origin in savagery, and they naturally appealed to peoples in whom the savage instincts were still strong[1]."

Among the Romans, under the Empire and onwards, this worship became prominent, and was still existent in the 4th century, for Symmachus tells of the celebrations of the festivals of Magna Mater[2]. Its special feature was the orgiastic dance of the priests[3], accom-

[1] Frazer, *GB, Adonis, Attis, and Osiris*, pp. 250 f. (1907). See further, Hepding, *Attis, seine Mythen und sein Kult*, pp. 128 ff. (1903).
[2] *Ep.* I. 49, II. 34, VI. 40; Dill, *Roman Society in the last century of the Western Empire*, p. 16 (1910).
[3] On the Galli see Lucian, *De Dea Syria*, XLIII, L–LX.

panied by song, which culminated in self-laceration. The third day of this festival of Kybele and Attis was known as the Day of Blood (*Dies Sanguinis*); the Archigallus or high-priest drew blood from his arms and presented it as an offering. Nor was he alone in making this bloody sacrifice:

Stirred by the wild barbaric music of clashing cymbals, rumbling drums, droning horns, and screaming flutes, the inferior clergy whirled about in the dance with waggling heads and streaming hair, until, rapt in a frenzy of excitement, and insensible to pain, they gashed their bodies with potsherds or slashed them with knives in order to bespatter the altar and the sacred tree with their flowing blood[1].

Thus, while among the Romans during the early centuries of the Christian era, and owing to the influx of oriental cults, the ecstatic dance in its most barbaric form was prominent, among the Greeks this form of it made but little appeal, and it is only rarely that reference is made to it. But although this extreme and sanguinary form was distasteful to the Greeks, the ecstatic dance was with them of a very wild character; and it is possible that the *purpose* of this type of dance among Greeks and Romans respectively may have had something to do with its form. Reference is made to this point below (see p. 138), but we must first take a brief glance at the ecstatic dance as practised among some of the uncultured races.

[1] Frazer, *op. cit.* p. 223. See further Cicero, *De Divinatione*, II. 50; Catullus, *Carm.* LXIII.; Lucretius, II. 598 ff.; Hepding, *op. cit.*, pp. 142 ff.; Glover, *The Conflict of Religions in the early Roman Empire*, pp. 20 f. (1909).

IV

Among uncultured peoples the ecstatic dance appears both in its milder and its more barbaric forms. To take a few examples of the former first.

The means employed to become "possessed" are various, but the most usual is the dance accompanied by the rhythmic beating of a drum or other instrument; this is persisted in until with the rising excitement it becomes wilder and wilder, and ultimately brings about unconsciousness, or at least semi-consciousness, in the dancer. Thus, the Vedda form of "possession" is attained by a dance which began with moderate movements in which "the shaman, while uttering invocations to the spirits, circles round the offerings; the dance increases in speed until the seizure takes place[1]." Again, in Southern India we have the example of the so-called "devil-dancers," who work themselves into paroxysms in order to gain inspiration,

whereby they profess to cure their patients. So, with furious dancing to music and chanting of the attendants the Bodo priest brings on a fit of maniacal inspiration in which the deity fills him and gives oracles through him[2].

Another instructive instance is that of the Tshi-speaking peoples of the Gold Coast whose priests and priestesses are believed to be from time to time

possessed or inspired by the deity whom they serve; and in that state they are consulted as oracles. They work themselves up to the necessary pitch of excitement by dancing to the music of drums; each god has his

---

[1] Fallaize, in *ERE*, x. 124 *b*.

[2] Tylor, *Primitive Culture*, II. 133 f. (1920); he also mentions this type of dance among the Patagonians, Fijians and others, pp. 419 ff.

special hymn, sung to a special beat of the drums, and accompanied by a special dance. It is while thus dancing to the drums that the priest or priestess lets fall the oracular words in a croaking or guttural voice which the hearers take to be the voice of the god. Hence dancing has an important place in the education of priests and priestesses; they are trained in it for months before they may perform in public. These mouth-pieces of the deity are consulted in almost every concern of life, and are handsomely paid for their services[1].

Among the North American Indians with whom the sacred dance acts as the expression of religious feeling to a greater degree than perhaps among any other un-cultured races with the exception of the aborigines of Oceania, dancing to the point of unconsciousness is an act of devotion to the god[2].

This is further illustrated by the ancient Peruvians; among them the religious dance was "the grand form of religious demonstration." The very name of their principal festivals, *Raymi*, means "dance." Their dances at these festivals are of such a violent character that the dancers seem to be out of their senses. "It is note-worthy," says Réville, "that the Incas themselves took no part in the violent dances, but had an 'Incas' dance of their own, which was grave and measured[3]."

Another example, offered by Skeat, is from a very different centre. In writing about dances among the Malays, which, as he says, are almost all religious in their origin, he goes on to tell of one which "began soberly like the others, but grew to a wild revel until

---

[1] Frazer, *GB*, *Adonis, Attis, Osiris*, p. 61.
[2] Réville, *Les Religions des peuples non-civilisés*, p. 267 (1883); Schoolcraft, *op. cit.* i. 286.
[3] *Native Religions of Mexico and Peru* (Hibbert Lectures, 1884), p. 225.

the dancers were, or pretended to be, possessed by the Spirit of Dancing, *hantu měnāri* as they called it...[1]."

Lastly, in Borneo the Kayan medicine-women, in the course of exorcism of the evil spirit for the cure of disease, whirl round until they fall in a faint[2].

A modern European example of this type of dance is that performed among some Russian sectaries; in order to produce a state of religious exaltation wild, whirling dances, like those of the dancing dervishes, are executed[3].

These are but a very few examples of many which could be given; but they are sufficient to answer our purposes.

Before coming to one or two illustrations of the more barbaric form of this type of dance, one instance may be offered of the ecstatic dance of the milder kind being performed with an object different from those which are usually connected with it. Among the Maoris the war-dance, which was looked upon as a religious act, was often performed on the eve of battle in order to impart daring and bravery to the warriors; and this dance often assumed the form of frenzy when accompanied by the beating of drums and the shouting of the dancers. An eye-witness describes it thus:

> The Maoris turned their faces into close imitations of their demonlike carved images. But the thrust-out tongue, the wild rolling eyes standing out of the head, the fierce grimaces, and the quivering hands and fingers, with the accompaniment of the deep-drawn cries and the stamp of feet, had all the advantages of living move-

---

[1] *Malay Magic*, p. 463 (1900).   [2] Fallaize, in *ERE*, x. 124 *b*.
[3] Frazer, *GB*, *The Magic Art*, i. 408; N. Tsaki, *La Russie Sectaire*, pp. 66 ff. The Shakers of New Lebanon attempt in the dance to obtain the Holy Spirit, Lilly Grove, *op. cit.* p. 7.

ment to add to the terrifying effect. It is difficult to efface the deep impression that its massive energy and furious, almost epileptic, passion makes on the mind, when produced by hundreds. It surpassed in fury anything that kava or any other drug or fermented liquor could have given to the harmonious movements of a mass of warriors[1].

Strictly speaking, this hardly belongs to the category of ecstatic dances because it is not performed with any idea of communication with a supernatural power, whether as a means of effecting union with it, or honouring it, or as a form of supplication to it; nevertheless, it is worth recording here, if only because it affords an illustration of the extended use of a rite for purposes with which originally it had nothing to do.

And now to give, finally, an example or two of the ecstatic dance in its most extreme and barbaric form. Frazer tells us that

when game was very scarce, certain Basuto tribes which lived partly by the chase, were wont to assemble and invoke the spirit of a famous dead chief and other ancestral deities. At these ceremonies they cut themselves with knives, rolled in ashes, and uttered piercing cries. They also joined in religious dances, chanted plaintive airs, and gave vent to loud lamentations. After spending a whole day and night in wailing and prayer, they dispersed next morning to scour the country in search of the game which they confidently expected the ghosts or gods would send in answer to their intercession[2].

He compares this with the frenzied rites of the Canaanite prophets of Baal, and refers to another well-known case among the Israelites themselves (Hos. vii. 14), in which

---

[1] J. Macmillan Brown, *Maori and Polynesian*, p. 204 (1907).
[2] *Folklore in the Old Testament*, iii. 277 (1918).

they lacerated their bodies by way of appealing to the
deity on behalf of their corn and vines. The non-mention
of the sacred dance in this passage does not imply that
it did not take place; analogies suggest that it was an
indispensable part of the rite.

Another instructive example is given by Jevons which
he takes from Bishop Caldwell's "very careful observations in Tinnevelly[1]." He says:

In Tinnevelly evil spirits have no regular priests; but
when it becomes necessary, in consequence of some
pressing need, to resort to the aid of these spirits, some
one is chosen, or offers himself, to be the priest for the
occasion, and is dressed up in the insignia of the spirit.
As blood is the sacrifice to a god, so in the dance with
which the evil spirits, like the tribal god, are worshipped,
the dancer in an ecstasy draws his own blood and drinks
that of the victim, a goat, say, and thus the spirit passes
into him, and he has the power of prophecy. As the
sacrifice of the sacred victims was a solemn mystery to
be celebrated by night, and terminated before sunrise,
so the worship of the evil spirits must be performed by
night, and the general opinion is that night is the
appropriate time for their worship[2].

Here we have another interesting parallel to the procedure of the priests of Baal, though, as the Canaanite
worship had reached, in comparison, a higher stage, the
parallel does not hold good in all particulars. But we
have the pressing need of the Baal-worshippers, the
sacrifice to the god, the dance round the altar, the
dancers in an ecstasy drawing their own blood, and the
spirit of prophecy passing into them[3]; the sacrifice takes

[1] In *Allerlei*, I. 164–168.
[2] *Introduction to the Study of Religion*, p. 174 (1904).
[3] "They prophesied until the time of the evening oblation"
(עֲלוֹת הַמִּנְחָה), 1 Kings xviii. 29.

place after sunset. They do not drink the blood of the sacrificial victim in order to become possessed by the god because this is effected by means of the ecstatic dance whereby they prophesy; and probably this points to an advance in religious conception; for the belief that union is effected by the ecstatic dance is certainly not so crass and materialistic as that which requires the essence of the deity to pass into his worshippers by drinking the blood of the sacrificial victim offered to him, and which is supposed to become identified with the god. In other respects the parallel is sufficiently striking. In each case it is clear that the ecstatic dance is an essential part of the ritual.

The pressing needs which this type of sacrifice with its ecstatic dance are supposed to supply are various, but there is a curious and instructive similarity in most of the details of the ritual wherever it is practised, showing that the underlying ideas are generally the same in every case. Here is one more example. In his book on Serpent-worship in India Mr C. F. Oldham describes what he saw during the great sacrifice to *Kailang Nāg*, which was celebrated in the village of the Ravi, and which had for its object the obtaining of fine weather for the sowing,—this had been delayed owing to storms. *Kailang*, a demi-god, is supposed to control the weather. The writer says:

On my arrival I found the people assembled on the open grassy space in front of the temple. The men and the boys sat together, the women and the girls being at a little distance. Soon the music struck up, and some of the men and boys began to dance in a circle, the *chela*[1] dancing in the centre. After a time the music

[1] An inspired prophet.

became wilder and the dance more energetic. Some of the men, when tired, sat down, and others took their places. The *chela* continued dancing, and he applied the *sungal*[1] to his own back and shoulders, and to those of some of the other dancers. Some of the men then applied another similar scourge to their backs, with great effect, amid shouts of *Kailang Mahārāi ki jāi* ("Victory to the great king Kailang"). Then, all being ready, a victim (a ram) was led out, and having shown, by shivering, that it was acceptable to the deity, its head was struck off. The body was immediately lifted up by several men, and the *chela*, seizing upon it, drank the blood as it spouted from the neck, amid renewed shouts of *Kailang Mahārāi ki jāi*. The carcase was thrown down upon the ground, and the head, with a burning coal upon it, placed before the threshold of the temple. The dancing was then renewed, and became more violent, until the *chela* gasped out *Kailang āya* ("Kailang has come"). All then became silent, and the prophet announced that the sacrifice was accepted, and that the season would be favourable. This was received with a storm of shouts of *Kailang Mahārāi ki jāi*, and the *chela* sank down upon the ground exhausted. Water was poured over him, and he was vigorously fanned till he showed signs of revival. The assembly then began to disperse[2].

These three examples exhibit essentially the same *traits* and sufficiently illustrate this type of dance in its extreme form among peoples of low civilization, so that it is unnecessary to multiply illustrations. It must, however, be said that this more barbarous form of the ecstatic dance is not nearly so prevalent as the form previously mentioned; it seems to be resorted to in times of emer-

---

[1] A five-thonged scourge, with iron at the extremity of each thong.

[2] *The Sun and the Serpent*, pp. 99 f. (1905).

gency, and in this offers a further parallel to the case
of the prophets of Baal.

*   *   *   *

SUMMARY AND CONSIDERATIONS

The ecstatic dance is performed as the outcome of
strong religious emotion; it begins quietly and without
any indication of what is to come; but the intention to
increase it gradually to an extravagant pitch is there
from the commencement, and it continues until semi-
consciousness, and even total unconsciousness is reached.
The excitement caused by the dance frequently becomes
contagious, so that others join in. The purpose of this
dance is to effect union with a superhuman spirit; the
body, temporarily "emptied" of consciousness, is believed to be entered by the god or spirit in whose honour
the dance takes place. Among peoples of low culture,
among whom belief in the "external soul" is common,
there can be no doubt that the conviction existed that
the soul took its departure from the body for the
time being, thus making room for the higher spirit
of the god. While thus inhabiting the body, the god
utilized it for his own purposes. The prime motive
of the ecstatic dance was union with the deity; that
being once effected other things might or might not
follow.

The ecstatic dance takes, however, a different form,
and has a different purpose under special circumstances.
It acts sometimes as a means of forcing the deity (or,
rather, it is believed to do so) to answer prayer; then
during the ecstatic state self-laceration takes place,

apparently with little or no sensation of pain; the loss of consciousness does not necessarily ensue. Both these forms of the ecstatic dance are met with among the Israelites. The former was practised by the prophets, and its contagious character is forcibly illustrated; as a result the spirit of Jahwe comes upon the performer. The latter is mentioned as a Syrian rite practised in time of emergency by the prophets of Baal; but the influence of Syrian, or Canaanite, practice upon the Israelites here is plainly indicated by the prophet Hosea who tells of how the people "cut themselves for corn and wine," thus rebelling against their God. Though in this instance the dance is not mentioned we know from the parallel case of the prophets of Baal that it was part of the ritual, and therefore took place; and this quite apart from the analogous practice elsewhere. It was done with the purpose of forcing the god (in this case some local Baal) to give good crops. It was, so we may believe, an emergency rite; the more normal method may have been the dance round the sacred tree (see above, pp. 96, 99, 103). As to the special form of dance on these occasions, it is probable, so far as the prophetic dance was concerned, that it began in quite moderate style, and in single file formation; as the excitement increased it is obvious that it assumed a very different form, a whirling round with head thrown back, judging from analogy. In the case of the wilder, Syrian, form, there is reason to suppose that it began also quietly, with the "limping" step, and presently got wilder and wilder, until knives and other sharp instruments were seized, and self-inflicted wounds caused blood to flow from the bodies of the performers. The purpose of the "limping" step is believed, with good reason, to have been to arouse the pity of the god, or else to imitate him and thus induce him to hear the prayers addressed to him; the flowing blood may be regarded as having been a means of forcing the god to answer prayer.

The ecstatic dance, at any rate in its more barbarous form, is unknown among other Semitic peoples. This holds good also of the Egyptians, though the present day existence of it, in its less barbarous form, among the Dancing Dervishes supports the belief of its having been in vogue in earlier times.

With regard to the Syrians, however, there is the clearest evidence of its existence in both forms; for we have the story of Wen-Amon, and the detailed accounts of Heliodorus and Apuleius.

Very full evidence is forthcoming as to the ecstatic dance among the Greeks; it is, however, not indigenous, and can be shown to have come to them from the Syrians. It is, in the main, connected with the worship of Dionysos, in whose honour the Thyiads danced and raved, often until they became insensible. The god was supposed to be present at the orgies which took place during his festivals, and those who, by means of orgiastic dances, lost consciousness, came under his influence and were "possessed" by him. The instances of this dance among the Greeks, of which some notable ones are recorded above, show to what an extent it was in vogue; but we find that, in general, it is the less barbarous form of the ecstatic dance that was performed among them. The more objectionable form was rare; it occurred in connexion with the worship of Attis, but this was not popular among the Greeks. On the other hand, strange to say, among the Romans, especially during the later period of the Empire and owing to the influx of alien oriental cults, this form of worship became prominent. National characteristics undoubtedly had much to do with this contrast between Greeks and Romans; but it is probable that the respective purposes of the dance also had something to do with it; for while the main purpose of the ecstatic dance among the Greeks was to bring about the union of the god with his worshippers, among the Romans it appears to have been that of offering their blood. Among the Greeks, that is to say, it was in the nature of an act of devotion; but among the Romans it was to induce the goddess of fertility to give abundant crops.

Both forms of this dance appear among uncultured peoples. Its purpose is "possession" during which the possessed becomes endowed with supernatural powers; he is able to cure diseases, or to give oracles; or else it is purely an act of devotion. Among the Maoris it is supposed to have the effect of imparting courage, so it is performed on the eve of battle.

In its more barbaric form it is supposed to induce the higher powers to supply wants, as among the Basutos when game is scarce. An interesting example of the rite is offered by the natives in Tinnevelly in which both union with a supernatural being, and the power of prophecy is attained by means of this type of dance; it is true that, among these natives the actual union with the spirit is effected by offering him blood and drinking that of the victim sacrificed to the spirit; but the necessary spiritual condition into which the worshipper must be transported for this purpose is brought about through the sacred dance. But in this instance, as invariably among the uncivilized races, there is always some practical end in view; a material need of some kind arises which, it is believed, will be supplied by means of this rite.

In comparing this type of dance, as practised among many peoples, with the three instances of it given in the Old Testament, it will have been seen that there is a striking similarity both in purpose and performance. It is noteworthy, however, that among the Hebrews it is the milder type that is indigenous, and it is essentially an act of devotion; it is a means of receiving the spirit of Jahwe, and this for the practical purpose of divining His will and proclaiming it. The rite as practised by the prophets of Baal is Syrian; and there can be little doubt that the custom recorded by Hosea was of Syrian origin. So that, as among the Greeks, the milder form of the ecstatic dance was indigenous, while the more barbarous form was due to Syrian influence.

Reviewing the subject as a whole, there is no shadow of doubt that Hebrew and Greek practice here, though it is but a small item of religious ritual with which we have been concerned, illustrates their religious superiority over all the other races. But of these two the Hebrews stand on distinctly higher ground; there is not the remotest reason for believing that the ecstatic dance among them was ever contaminated by the licence which often obtained among the Greeks. Among the Hebrews, moreover, the object of it was purely devotional; and when an oracle was put forth it was only to declare the will of their God. So that it is true to say that even in the lower planes of religious thought and practice the Hebrews showed that they were in the vanguard of religious evolution.

CHAPTER VIII

THE SACRED DANCE AT VINTAGE, HARVEST, AND OTHER FESTIVALS

I

W E are not concerned here with the history and development of the Hebrew feasts; but a few introductory words regarding them will not be out of place.

There were three agricultural festivals of first importance among the Israelites:

Mazzôth[1], or the feast of Unleavened Bread; this was a spring feast held when the sickle was first put to the standing corn and the first-fruits of the new crops were offered (Deut. xvi. 8, 9);

Shabuôth, or the feast of Weeks, celebrated seven weeks later at the conclusion of the harvest (Deut. xvi. 10); called also *Ḳazir*, the feast of "Harvest" (Exod. xxiii. 16);

Sukkôth, or the feast of Tabernacles, the autumn feast, called also *ha-Asiph*, the feast of "the ingathering," when "thou gatherest in thy labours out of the field" (Exod. xxiii. 16).

Since prior to their entry into Canaan the Israelites were nomads, and therefore did not observe harvest festivals, it is extremely probable that, in settling down among the Canaanites, they adopted these festivals from the people of the land, and celebrated them in honour of Jahwe, their God.

---

[1] The feast of *Pesach* ("Passover") coincided with this; it was also a spring festival at which the firstlings of the herds were offered (Exod. xxxiv. 25).

These three great feasts were originally, among the
Israelites, of equal importance, requiring presence at the
sanctuary (Exod. xxxiv. 23); but there are indications
that in quite early times the autumn feast of Tabernacles
assumed pre-eminence. It is called "the feast," or "the
feast of Jahwe[1]." The other feasts were celebrated
locally.

From the present point of view it is important to note
that each of these feasts is called *ḥag*: *ḥag ha-Mazzôth,
ḥag ha-Kazir, ḥag ha-Asiph*; that is to say, to each is
applied the term which originally denoted what was the
essence of a festival, viz. the sacred dance round the
sanctuary; and the same is true of the minor festivals
which were celebrated at the local sanctuaries.

In view of the fact that the feast was called *ḥag* because of the sacred dance characteristic of it, no surprise
can be felt at the non-mention of dancing at these feasts
when they are spoken of in the Old Testament; it was
so obvious and customary that any reference to it, excepting incidental allusions, would have been quite
superfluous[2]. Such incidental allusions occur in the
Psalms, as we have seen, and a more specific mention
is met with in Judg. xi. 34: "And Jephthah came to
Mizpah unto his house, and, behold, his daughter came
out to meet him with timbrels and with dances"; we
are not here concerned with the character of the feast
referred to[3]; our point is that it was celebrated with

---

[1] *E.g.* 1 Kings viii. 2, xii. 32; Judg. xxi. 19; Lev. xxiii. 39, 41.
[2] This is also true of the Targums, where an allusion to the
dance is sometimes strikingly obvious, *e.g.* in the Targ. of *Onkelos*
to Deut. xvi. 14; the people are bidden to rejoice at their feasts
with the playing of flutes; this was one of the most usual accom-
paniments to the sacred dance all the world over.
[3] See Moore, *Judges*, pp. 304 f. (1903).

dancing. Another and fuller illustration occurs in Judg. xxi. 19 ff., where mention is made of a feast which was held annually at Shiloh in honour of Jahwe; that it was a vintage feast is implied by the reference to the vineyards in which the Benjamites hid themselves[1]. At this feast it was the custom for the young girls to come out and dance: "When the maidens of Shiloh come out to dance in the dances"; and see verse 23. It is worth noticing how the dancing is mentioned as a recognized custom. The spot must have been a familiar one as the feast took place annually; we are reminded of *Abel-meḥolah*, "the field of dancing" (1 Kings xix. 16), which must clearly have got its name from the festival dancing which took place there habitually.

We know from the later history and ritual of the Jewish festivals that they were marked by dances and processional dances of a sacred character[2]; and the analogy of ritual usage among other peoples makes it certain that these religious dances at the Jewish feasts, as practised in post-biblical times, were not innovations, but rather the traditional ritual which had been handed down from time immemorial. As Krauss points out, the most primitive kind of dancing, a simple form of hopping, without rhythmic movement (for which the Talmud uses the word *taphaz*), was in use in later times both at weddings and during regular worship[3].

We have already, in another connexion, drawn attention to the daily procession round the altar, after the sacrifices had been offered, during the feast of *Sukkôth*

---

[1] Cp. Judges ix. 27.
[2] See *e.g.* Reinach, *Orpheus*, p. 273 (1909); Carl Rathjens, *Die Juden in Abessinien*, p. 78 (1921).
[3] *Talmudische Archäologie*, iii. 101, and the references on p. 285.

("Tabernacles"). There was another dancing ceremony
at this feast which must be mentioned, a ceremony of
which it was said that whosoever had not seen it had
never seen a real feast[1]. This was the wonderful Torch-
dance which took place in the Court of the women in
the Temple on the second day of the feast. A great
multitude of men and women were always present on
this occasion to witness the dance in which only the
most prominent among the Israelites took part. While
the dance was going on hymns and psalms were sung[2].
It was because of the dances and processions at the
feast of Tabernacles, during which palms and branches
of trees were carried, similar to the *thyrsus* carried
by the Bacchanalian assemblies of maidens, that Plutarch was betrayed into the error of regarding this feast
as of the same character as that celebrated in honour of
Dionysos among the Greeks; and into his assertion that
the cult of this god was in vogue among the Hebrews[3].

There was, to give another example, a religious dance,
though of an entirely different character, carried out by
Jewish maidens both on the feast-day known as the
15th of Ab, and on the Day of Atonement[4]. That the
feast of the 15th of Ab was a religious one is clear from
the evidence given by Rabbi Eliezer ben Hyrcanus[5]
(1st century A.D.) to the effect that it was the great day
of the year on which wood was offered for the burning
of the sacrifices; the supply offered on this occasion was
supposed to be sufficient to last for the year. The

---

[1] Mishnah, *Sukkah*, v. 1.   [2] *Sukkah*, iv. 1–4.
[3] Cp. Reinach, *op. cit.* p. 271.
[4] See *Megillath Taanith*, iv. 8–10; this was before the Day of
Atonement had become a Fast-day; one sees, therefore, how
ancient the custom was.
[5] *Megillath Taanith*, v.

144 THE SACRED DANCE AT VINTAGE,

festival is referred to by Josephus, who calls it the Xulophoria[1].

To mention but one further example, at the feast of *Purim* there was a special kind of dance; although this ceased to be of a religious character, there can be no doubt that originally it was so[2].

II

Among the ancient Arabs, being nomads, Harvest and Vintage festivals did not, of course, exist. But among their descendants a festival of another kind at which a dance of, at any rate, a quasi-religious character is performed may be mentioned here; for there can be no doubt that in these things modern usage represents a custom which has been handed down through the generations from the distant past. At circumcision festivals (*Muzzayîn*)[3] they perform what are called *Daḥa* dances. The young people gather together, being invited by the fathers of the children to be circumcised, and perform these dances, during which they sing over and over again:

> We will protect you
> From him who cuts (*'enda-l-Ḳatta'*)
> We will protect you.
> Cut, oh Cutter!
> Yet hurt not [here, in turn, the names of those who
>   are to be circumcised are uttered],
> Cut, oh Cutter!
> Beware of the reed (*'ala-l-Ḳaṣab*),
> Oh my darling,
> Beware of the reed![4]

[1] *Bell. Jud.* ii. xvii. 6.
[2] See further on this, Krauss, *op. cit.* iii. 102, 285.
[3] On these see further Doughty, *Travels in Arabia Deserta*, i. 340 ff., 391 f. (1921).
[4] Alois Musil, *Arabia Petraea*, iii. 200 ff. (1908).

Dancing at circumcisions is indispensable among the peasants in Palestine[1]; it has been observed also in many other parts of the world, e.g. among the Bambaras of Senegambia[2].

In Gen. xxi. 4, where the circumcision of Isaac is recorded, there is no mention of the circumcision feast and the accompanying dance, which, judging from later usage, always took place; but in verse 8 it says: "...And Abraham made a great feast on the day that Isaac was weaned." The Rabbis of later times inferred that just as there was a feast at the weaning there must also have been a feast at the circumcision, and no doubt they were right. In *Pirke de Rabbi Eliezer* we read in reference to this passage (Gen. xxi. 4): "The sages said: A man is bound to make festivities and a banquet on that day when he has the merit of having his son circumcised, like Abraham our Father, who circumcised his son, as it is said...[3]." That dancing formed an indispensable element at such feasts, as among other peoples who practised this rite, hardly admits of doubt[4]. In most cases, though not in all, there enters in a distinctly religious note.

There is also dancing at the festivities attending the performance of vows[5].

III

Although it is highly probable that at the Harvest and other festivals of the Babylonians and Assyrians sacred dancing took place, definite evidence in the way of recorded instances does not seem to be forthcoming.

[1] Dalman, *Palestinischer Diwan*, p. 254 (1901).
[2] Featherman, *Social History of Mankind*, i. 334 f. (1881).
[3] See G. Friedlander's edition of this work, p. 208 (1916).
[4] Cp. Enclow, *JE*, iv. 425 b, and Jacobs, *JE*, iv. 96 ff.
[5] See Curtiss, *op. cit.* pp. 164 ff.

Among the Egyptians, however, we know that every
temple had both priests and priestesses attached, among
whom were dancers and musicians; and these played a
very important part at all festivals[1]. Apart from official
celebrations in temples, local feasts at which sacred
dances were performed, also took place. Thus, when the
Harvest was completed and the peasants offered the
first-fruits, they danced in the presence of the god of
fertility as an act of thanksgiving[2]. There was also a
dance of thanksgiving performed in honour of Ptah for
the annual overflowing of the Nile. In dancing a small
piece of wood was often held in each hand, and these
were knocked together in rhythmic time[3].

Mention should also be made of the great "Sed"
festival, originally performed only once in thirty years,
but later in every third year. At this festival the king
was deified as Osiris, and the Crown Prince was ap-
pointed, and married to the heiress of the kingdom. At
the enthronization of the deified king the Crown Prince
danced before him as an act of honour to the god; this
was also done at another part of the ceremony by all
the men, who were present in great numbers[4].

IV

A good example among the Greeks is that of the sacred

[1] Kees, *Der Opfertanz des ägyptischen Königs*, pp. 105–226
(1912); Maspero, *Études de mythologie et de l'archéologie égyp-
tiennes*, VIII. 313 (1893–1916); Blackman, *Rock Tombs of Meir*,
I. 23 f., II. 25, and the same writer in the *Journal of Egyptian
Archaeology*, VII. 21 f.

[2] Erman, *Aegypten...*, I. 336.

[3] Erman, *op. cit.* I. 340; see also Voss, *Der Tanz und seine
Geschichte*, p. 20 (1869), who unfortunately omits references to
authorities.

[4] See further, Flinders Petrie, *Stud. Hist.* III. 69 (1904), and for
festivals generally the same author's *Egyptian Festivals...* (1908).

dance performed at the celebration of the *Haloa*, which, according to a scholion to Lucian[1], was

a feast at Athens containing mysteries of Demeter, and Kore, and Dionysos on the occasion of the cutting of vines and the tasting of wine made from them....The *Haloa* gets its name, according to Philochorus, from the fact that people hold sports at the *threshing-floors*; and he says it is celebrated in the month Poseidon[2]....The sports held were, of course, incidental to the business of threshing; but it was these sports that constituted the actual festival. To this day the great round threshing-floor that is found in most Greek villages is the scene of the harvest festival. Near it a booth (*skēnē*) is to this day erected, and in it the performers rest, and eat and drink in the intervals of their pantomimic dancing[3].

In connexion with ritual dances in honour of Demeter, Frazer draws attention to the remains of "the magnificent marble drapery which once adorned the colossal statue of Demeter and Persephone in the sanctuary of the two goddesses at Lycosura, in Arcadia"; on this are carved rows of semi-human, semi-bestial figures dancing and playing musical instruments; the bodies of these figures are those of women, but their heads, paws and feet are those of a horse, a pig, a cat, or a hare, and apparently an ass[4].

"It is reasonable to suppose," he says, "that these dancing figures represent a ritual dance which was

[1] *Schol. in Luc. Dialog. Meretr.* vii. 4 (ed. Rabe, 1906), referred to by Harrison, *op. cit.* p. 146; see also Lübker, *op. cit.* 298 *b*.

[2] Mommsen, *Feste...*, pp. 359 ff.; Harpocration, *s.v.* Ἁλῷα, i. 24 (ed. Dindorf [1853]). For Vintage Festivals see, further, Mommsen, *Heortologie*, pp. 66 ff.

[3] Harrison, *op. cit.* pp. 146 f. On this festival see also Bekker, *op. cit.* i. 384 f.; Farnell, *Cults...*, iii. 315 f.; Frazer, *GB*, *The Spirits of the Corn and of the Wild*, i. 60 ff.

[4] The author refers to his note on Pausanias, viii. xxxvii. 3 in vol. iv. pp. 375 ff. of his *Pausanias*.

actually performed in the rites of Demeter and Persephone by masked men and women, who personated the goddesses in their character of beasts[1]."

The story of the two daughters of Eteokles who fell into a well while dancing in honour of Demeter and Kore, and were turned into cypresses, probably owes its origin to the desire to account for the reason why sacred dances were performed under these trees, in which the *numen* of one or other of these goddesses was supposed to reside[2]. The story is given in *Geoponica*, XI. 4:

The cypresses have two names, and they are indeed called *Charites* on account of their delectable quality, and *Cypresses* on account of their bearing and producing branches and seeds in such regular order. They were the daughters of Eteokles; and when dancing in imitation of the goddesses, they fell into a well; and the earth, commiserating their misfortune, produced flourishing plants like damsels[3].

It is unnecessary to give further examples; generally speaking, among the Greeks dancing at festivals, so far as their religious character is concerned, was performed in honour of some deity. A magical purpose is sometimes to be discerned, though rarely[4]; the ecstatic dance seems sometimes to have had this object, and this, as one

[1] *GB, Spirits of the Corn and of the Wild*, II. 339.
[2] Gruppe, *op. cit.* II. 783; Preller, *Griechische Mythologie*, pp. 618 ff. (1872).
[3] Cp. Pausan. VIII. xxv. 1 ff.; Ovid, *Metam.* v. 106; Pliny, XVI. 33; and for the *Charites* see Gruppe, *op. cit.* I. 81, II. 1073, 1083, 1189, 1284; Lobeck, *op. cit.* II. 1085 ff.; *Julii Pol. Onom.* IV. 95. For the Thesmophoria see Frazer, *GB, Spirits of the Corn...*, II. 16 ff.; Farnell, *Cults...*, III. 85–93; and for the Thargelia, *GB, The Scapegoat*, pp. 254 ff.; Farnell, *Cults...*, IV. 268 ff.
[4] *E.g.* in the cult of Ἄρτεμις Κορδάκα, see Lobeck, *De myst. priv.* II. 959; Farnell, *Cults...*, II. 445; Pausan. VI. xxii. 1. The procession called φαλλοφορία was especially associated with Dionysos and Hermes, see Farnell in *ERE*, VI. 417 a.

would expect, is only the case in the earliest period of Greek religion[1]. We have dealt in Chap. VII with the ecstatic dance and its objects.

V

As illustrating this type of dance among the Romans we may instance the festival of the *Ambarvalia*; this festival was not celebrated on a fixed date, but varied according to the state of the crops. The duties at the festival were carried out by *Fratres Arvales*, "the Brethren of the Ploughed Fields." With solemn prayers, addressed primarily to Mars[2] to keep away all harm from the crops, these Brethren led round in formal procession the victims destined for sacrifice to Mars as the god of vegetation, viz. a pig, a ram, and a bull. The Arval Brothers had a special three-step dance (*tripudium*) which they performed in honour of Mars and the Lares; it was repeated three times, and during its performance they sang a hymn of praise to the god[3]. A minute account of their three days' festival is given in the *Acta* of the year 218 (Elagabalus, *CIL*, VI. 2104)[4]; the dance, which took place on the second, and most important, day is described as follows: "...Then the priests, shut up in the temple, girding up their togas, took the song-books and, marking the time, danced the three step singing thus...[5]." Again, at the festival of the *Lupercalia*, held in February, when the sacrificial

[1] See Farnell in *ERE*, VI. 403 *b*; he says: "this privilege of ecstasy might be used for the practical purposes of vegetation-magic."

[2] Mars was originally a god of vegetation; he appears subsequently as the god of war.

[3] See Aust, *Die Religion der Römer*, p. 171 (1899).

[4] A translation in full is given by Carter in *ERE*, II. 10 *b*, 11 *a*.

[5] See further on the whole subject Pauly-Wissowa, *Realencycl. der klassischen Altertumswissenschaft*, II. 1463 ff. (1896).

feast was ended, the *Luperci*, crowned and anointed, and, but for an apron of goatskin, entirely naked, ran round the Palatine Hill with thongs cut from the skin of the sacrificed goats in their hands[1]. The feast was held in honour of Faunus (the Greek Pan), who was worshipped under the name of Lupercus, in a grotto in the Palatine Mount called the Lupercal. The running round of the *Luperci* with the goats' thongs had a purificatory object[2] (see p. 101).

The dances of the *Salii* may be appropriately mentioned here. Their sacred processions took place in March and October, and continued for over three weeks[3]. Headed by trumpeters and dressed in full battle apparel they marched through the city; at all the altars and temples they halted, and, under the conduct of two leaders, solemnly danced the war-dance in three measures in honour of Mars, singing at the same time[4]. The *Salii*, however, also performed dances in honour of Saturn, the Roman god of sowing;

"as the Romans," says Frazer, "sowed the corn both in spring and autumn, and as down to the present time in Europe superstitious rustics are wont to dance and leap high in the spring for the purpose of making the crops grow high, we may conjecture that the leaps and dancing performed by the *Salii*, the priests of the old Italian god of vegetation, were similarly supposed to

[1] See Marquardt, *Römische Staatsverwaltung*, iii. 444 (1885).
[2] Cp. the name of the month in which the festival was held, February, which gets its name from *februare* "to purify."
[3] March 19 was a special day as being the birthday of Minerva (Ovid, *Fasti*, iii. 812; see Mommsen, *Feste...*, p. 59).
[4] "...per urbem ire canentes carmina cum tripudiis solemnique saltatu," Liv. i. 20. 4. See, further, Wissowa, *op. cit.* i. 482, who refers to Dion. Hal. ii. 70. 2. Cp. de la Saussaye, *op. cit.* ii. 441 ff.; and see Seneca, *Epp.* xv; Quintilian, i. 2. 18.

quicken the growth of the corn by homoeopathic or imitative magic[1]."

It was not in Rome alone that this type of dancing was performed; similar colleges of dancing priests are known to have existed in many towns of ancient Italy, and everywhere, we may conjecture, they were supposed to contribute to the fertility of the earth by their leaps and dances[2]. This magical purpose of the sacred dance will come before us again.

VI

A few examples of this type of the sacred dance among uncultured peoples may now be given[3].

The sowing festival among the Kayans of Central Borneo, who are essentially an agricultural people and of a primitive type, is very elaborate; but we are only concerned with that part of it at which the sacred dancing takes place. The following is taken from an eye-witness' account:

The first to appear on the scene were some men wearing wooden masks and helmets and so thickly wrapt in banana leaves that they looked like moving masses of green foliage. They danced silently, keeping time to the beat of the gongs. They were followed by other figures, some of whom executed war-dances; but the

[1] *GB, The Scapegoat*, p. 232.
[2] Frazer, *ibid.*; Marquardt, *Römische Staatsverwaltung*, III. 427 f. (1885); Aust, *op. cit.* p. 130; Cirilli, *Les Prêtres Danseurs de Rome*, pp. 97 ff. (1913); for Harvest Festivals generally among the Romans see Wissowa, *Religion und Kultus der Römer*, pp. 191 ff., for the *Hilaria*, pp. 321 ff. (1912); Roscher, *Ausführliches Lexikon der griechischen und römischen Mythologie*, s.v. Attis, I. 715 ff. (1884); for the *Vinalia*, Aust, *op. cit.* p. 173. Cp. Farnell, *The Evolution of Religion*, p. 145 (1905).
[3] See, for illustrations not mentioned here, Lilly Grove, *op. cit.* pp. 65–92.

weight of their leafy envelope was such that they soon grew tired, and though they leaped high, they uttered none of the wild war-whoops which usually accompany these martial exercises. When darkness fell the dances ceased and were replaced by a little drama representing a boar brought to bay by a pack of hounds....Later in the evening eight disguised girls danced, one behind the other, with slow steps and waving arms, to the glimmering light of torches and the strains of a sort of jew's harp[1].

Nieuwenhuis, who witnessed this, insists strongly on the religious character of all the festivals observed by these people. There can be little doubt that the dancing masked men represent the spirits of fertility; the high leaps are a magical rite to make the crops grow high; and the row of dancing girls waving their arms is probably in imitation of the field of healthy stalks swaying in the wind, and thus also an act of imitative magic. It is another form of the rite which is practised by the Kai of New Guinea who swing to and fro on reeds suspended from the branches of trees in order to promote the growth of the crops[2].

Among the Malays most of the dances seem to be for the purpose of amusement; but that some of them, at any rate, were originally of a religious character is evident from what Skeat says on the subject:

...All these dances, I was told, were symbolical; one of agriculture, with the tilling of the soil, the sowing of

[1] This is given by Frazer, *GB, Spirits of the Corn...*, I. 95 f., from A. W. Nieuwenhuis, *Quer durch Borneo*, I. 167–169 (1904...).

[2] Frazer, *op. cit.* p. 107. See also Chalmers, *Pioneering in New Guinea*, pp. 323 ff. H. L. Roth, *The Natives of Sarawak and British North Borneo*, I. 262 (1896), says: "The Dyaks really seem to consider dancing as a part of divine service, attributing to it some mysterious and wholesome efficacy";—they do not enquire why; it is taken for granted that it is so.

the seed, the reaping and winnowing of the grain, might easily have been guessed by the dancers' movements[1]. Such dances, as is well known, are always, in some stage of their development, connected with the worship of some god of vegetation[2]. Skeat says that

the religious origin of almost all Malay dances is still to be seen in the performance of such ritualistic observances as the burning of incense, the scattering of rice, and the invocation of the Dance-Spirit according to set forms, the spirit being exorcised (or "escorted homewards" as it is called) at the end of the performance[3].

One other example may be given, this time from Africa, of the dance being a propitiatory act, and accompanied by prayer; it takes place at moon festivals. The Hottentots (they are moon-worshippers) perform long nightly dances in honour of the moon, both at the appearance of the new moon and at full moon. After numberless strange contortions of the body which characterise these dances, and excruciating yells, the worshippers fling themselves to the ground; then they suddenly spring up, stamp about with their feet, and gaze up at the moon, crying: "Hail, see that we have honey, and that our flocks get plenty of food, and give us much milk!" Then the dancing, accompanied by the clapping of hands, continues. This goes on through the whole night with short pauses. According to some authorities the name Hottentot is derived from the noise

[1] *Malay Magic*, p. 462 (1900).
[2] Cp. Réville, *Les Religions des peuples non-civilisés*, p. 269, who tells of how the imitative magic dance develops into a specifically religious act.
[3] *Op. cit.* p. 464; see, further, pp. 465 ff., and also Skeat and Blagden, *Pagan Races of the Malay Peninsula*, I. 364 f., II. 119 ff., 126 ff., 137 with the illustration on p. 138; and for the negro Baris, whose country is situated on either bank of the White Nile, see Featherman, *Social History of the Races of Mankind*, I. 74 (1881).

made by their feet during these nightly sacred dances
at the moon festivals[1].

Examples could be multiplied to almost any extent;
those given are typical and they will suffice for present
purposes.

*   *   *   *

SUMMARY AND CONSIDERATIONS

A brief enumeration of the chief festivals among the
Israelites is called for in the present connexion because
they were agricultural feasts; and, as has already been
pointed out incidentally, one of the purposes of the
sacred dance was to ensure good crops. All that we
learn as to the character of these festivals in the Old
Testament emphasizes the element of rejoicing during
their celebration; and this applies with special force to
the feast of Tabernacles. The dancing which took place
at these feasts would, therefore, seem to have been
purely expressions of joy. But there are reasons for
believing that other elements entered in as well. Expressions of thanksgiving to a god are at the same time
a means of honouring him; and this, we may feel certain,
figured largely at the Israelite feasts; they were thankful
to Jahwe for the fruits of the field, and they were joyful
for plenty; so that when grateful joy expressed itself in
the dance it constituted an act of honouring, and therefore of worshipping, the national God. The rare explicit
mention of these dances during the feasts in the Old
Testament is easily accounted for.

But the cultural stage of the bulk of the Israelite
people, at the very least up to the time of the Exile,

[1] W. Schneider, *Die Religion der Afrikanischen Naturvölker*,
pp. 52–58 (1891); Fritsch, *Die Eingeborenen Süd-Afrika's*, p. 327
(1872).

can be proved by many indications in the Old Testament to have been no higher than other races; the extremely significant fact recorded by one of the prophets that, on occasion, the most barbarous form of the ecstatic dance, with its self-inflicted lacerations and blood-flowing, was practised by the people for the purpose of ensuring good crops, offers ample justification for the belief that one of the objects of the sacred dance at the spring festival was likewise to ensure good crops. The rite was a world-wide one, which is in itself presumptive evidence that it was practised by the Israelites.

The importance of the sacred dance during the Jewish feasts of later times, for the existence of which the evidence is ample, must be regarded as the observance of traditional custom.

The ancient Arabs did not cultivate the soil and therefore did not celebrate festivals of this kind. Among some modern Arabs dancing takes place at circumcision festivals, and it is accompanied by song; there are grounds for believing that the Israelites did the same. The dance in this case must be regarded as having been performed in honour of the newly initiated, who, by circumcision, were admitted into the community of the tribe[1].

Among the Egyptians both national and local Harvest festivals were celebrated; during these the sacred dance played an important part. We may take it that, as among the Israelites, the purpose of these dances was to express joyful gratitude to the god of fertility. The "Sed" festival was another occasion on which a sacred dance was performed; the deified king was honoured in this way.

[1] On initiation dances see Harrison, *Themis*, pp. 24 f.

The *Haloa* among the Greeks seems to have been at once a Harvest and Vintage festival; the dancing which took place during this feast must have been in honour of the god of fertility. In Greek villages at the present day the harvest festival takes place round the threshing-floor, and there is much dancing, but its old significance has now, of course, disappeared.

There is evidence that dances were performed in honour of the fertility goddess Demeter and Persephone; the dancers personated these goddesses in their character of beasts,—horses, pigs, etc.; while we have here a dance in honour of these divinities, it is possible that it also partook of the nature of imitative magic, it being a means of ensuring productivity.

An interesting case of framing a reason for the sacred dance under trees, the real reason being presumably forgotten, is that of the two daughters of Eteokles who were turned into cypresses; these were trees under which sacred dances were performed. Festival dances among the Greeks were often doubtless expressions of mirth and joy, but this did not prevent their being performed in honour of some deity; it was precisely similar among the Israelites to whom the exhortation was constantly given: "Ye shall rejoice before Jahwe your God," in connexion with the feasts (Lev. xxiii. 40, etc.). A magic-religious purpose is at times to be discerned in these Greek festival dances.

Among the Romans a notable instance of this type of sacred dance is that performed by "the Brethren of the Ploughed Fields"; they circled round the victims for sacrifice to Mars. A similar rite was carried out by the *Luperci* in honour of the god Faunus (the Greek Pan); it had a purificatory purpose. The dances of the

Salii were performed in honour of Mars; they also danced in honour of Saturn, the Roman god of sowing; their high leaps during the latter of these were believed to have the effect of making the corn grow high.

Among the uncultured races the Kayans of Central Borneo danced at their festivals with a purpose similar to that of the Romans; their high leaps were a magical rite to make the crops grow in height. A like result was believed by the Kai of New Guinea to be effected by swinging to and fro on reeds suspended from the branches of trees. The Malays perform imitative dances which at one time were believed to make the crops grow. Finally, the Hottentots dance in honour of the moon in belief that this will have the effect of prevailing upon their deity, the moon, to supply them and their flocks with sustenance.

We have no indications in the Old Testament that the sacred dances at the Israelite feasts had any other purpose than that of rejoicing before their God, and this was, of course, in the nature of honouring Him. But the possibility of the existence of imitative magic in connexion with them at some period of their history cannot be altogether excluded; this is suggested not only because the idea is so widespread, but also because even in much later times among the Jews we have an example of an imitative magical rite during a feast in the Temple. At the Feast of Tabernacles it was the custom for water to be drawn ceremonially by the priests from the fountain of Siloam; this was brought through the water-gate, when a long-drawn-out trumpet blast was sounded, into the Temple, where it was poured out upon the altar during the further blowing of trumpets; the rite was performed daily on the seven days of the Feast. That this was a piece of imitative magic for the purpose of ensuring a sufficient rainfall would suggest itself spontaneously; but we have the definite statement to this effect given by the Rabbis, for the object of the rite is explained by the words: "The Holy One, Blessed be He! said, Pour out water before me at the Feast, in order that the rains of the year may be blessed to you[1]." This clear evidence among the Jews for the existence of a magical rite to obtain rain is sufficient justification for believing that their forefathers may have performed dances at Harvest Festivals for the purpose of ensuring good crops.

[1] Bab. Talm. *Rosh Ha-shanah* 16 *a*, Mishnah, *Sukkah*, IV. 9; cp. Mishnah, *Berakôth*, v. 2; see also the curious story in Lucian, *De Dea Syria*, XIII; and for numbers of examples of rain-charms see Frazer, *GB*, *The Magic Art*, I. 247–329.

CHAPTER IX

DANCES IN CELEBRATION OF VICTORY

I

It is a natural and obvious thing that there should be expressions of joy on the occasion of victory; and, as dancing was one of the ways whereby joy was expressed, it is equally natural that this should have been performed on such occasions. Furthermore, when we find that in the records of these celebrations it is the women who do the dancing, this is only what is to be expected since it is done in honour of the victorious warriors. This is all in the natural order of things; and, so far as the Old Testament is concerned, it would seem that the simple recording of the fact that the celebration of a victory was one of the occasions on which dancing was performed is all that is required. However, this custom is widespread, and has been, and still is, in vogue among peoples in very different stages of culture; and in discussing a widespread custom, such as this, it is always possible that one may discern in the performance of it among less cultured races elements which suggest that originally there was something more in it than appears upon the surface. In other words, the possibility must be reckoned with that the custom as recorded in the Old Testament was in reality the survival of something which was believed to have a decisive effect in bringing about victory. The dance of the Israelite women on these occasions had a three-fold purpose; it was a means of expressing joy; it was also the way in which the victorious warriors were honoured; and, most important, it was an act of praise and thanksgiving to Jahwe; so that this type of dance was emphatically a religious one. If, as we hope to offer some grounds for believing, this type of dance was, in its origin, a means of effecting victory by magic, it will be an interesting illustration of magic being, as Mr Marett says, "part and parcel of the 'god-stuff' out of which religion fashions itself[1]."

In passing, it may be said that, in spite of the fact that the absence of the able-bodied men would make the women the natural performers in these kind of dances, this public appearance of oriental women witnesses to a very different condition of society from that with which we are familiar as obtaining in the East in later centuries; in other words, the Israelites were in some respects in a less advanced cultural stage than we are sometimes apt to suppose. Not that they were conscious of any other objects in this type of dance than those mentioned; we only mean that at this time immemorial custom, however different the reasons given for its existence, was more likely to be tenaciously held to than when radical changes in religious belief and social and moral conditions had taken place.

The type of dancing with which we are just now concerned has nothing to do with the war-dance, the primary aim of which

seems to be the development of physical excitement, and consequently courage, in the dancing warriors; secondarily, as magical ideas attach themselves, the aim of frightening the enemy by a demonstration of violence is added[2].

In the Old Testament there is no mention of the war-

---

[1] *The Threshold of Religion*, p. 76 (1909). [2] *ERE*, x. 359 *b*.

dance. But there was a solemn preparation for war, for it must be remembered that among the Israelites, as among other Semites, there was a religious element connected with the act of warfare. Warriors "consecrated" themselves before entering upon it (Isa. xiii. 3); the phrase for declaring war or entering upon a state of warfare is to "sanctify, or consecrate, war" (Mic. iii. 5, Jer. vi. 4); and battle was prepared for by sacrifice (1 Sam. xiii. 9, 10); moreover, after the battle the spoil, or part of it, was consecrated to Jahwe (1 Sam. xv. 21, 2 Sam. viii. 11, 1 Chron. xviii. 11).

The Israelites, thus, entered battle under the protection of Jahwe; the religious element, therefore, was strongly emphasized.

We proceed now to enumerate the instances in the Old Testament of dancing in celebration of victory.

In Exod. xv. 20, 21 a dance with song accompanied by musical instruments is performed by women in celebration of victory:

And Miriam the prophetess, the sister of Aaron, took a timbrel (*tôph*) in her hand; and all the women went out after her with timbrels and with dances. And Miriam chanted[1] to them,

Sing to Jahwe, for He is greatly exalted,
The horse and his rider hath He cast into the sea.

Here the dancing and singing have clearly the single purpose of thanksgiving to Jahwe, for the victory is ascribed solely to Him; so that the passage presents the highest development of purpose for which this type of dance was performed. It is the same in Ps. lxviii. 11, 12

---

[1] The root meaning of *'anah* is "to sing," see Isa. xxvi. 2, Exod. xxxii. 18, Ps. cxix. 172; and cp. the cognate Arabic root *ghanna*; in neo-Hebrew it is often used of singing in chorus.

(12, 13 in Hebr.), where there is an obvious reference to the custom: "Jahwe giveth the word, the women that publish the tidings (*i.e.* of victory) are a great host; kings of armies flee; and she that tarrieth at home divideth the spoil[1]." True, there is no mention of singing and dancing here; but if, as we may well believe, it was so well known that the women who celebrated the victory did sing and dance, there was no need to specify it.

In the example given in Judg. xi. 34 it is different, for the dancing and singing here are in honour of the victorious warrior. Jephthah, on his return from his victory over the Ammonites, is met by his daughter and other maidens (her companions are spoken of in verse 38) "with timbrels and with dances[2]." This is further illustrated by the well-known passage 1 Sam. xviii. 6, 7:

And it came to pass as they came, when David returned from the slaughter of the Philistines, that the women came out of the cities of Israel, singing and dancing, to meet king Saul, with timbrels, with joy and with instruments of music (*Shalishim*, whatever this may mean); and the dancing women sang to one another and said,

> Saul hath slain his thousands,
> And David his ten thousands.

The corruptions in the Hebrew text of this passage need not trouble us as they do not affect the special point with which we are concerned. The same event is referred to in 1 Sam. xxi. 11, where the way in which the

[1] A different interpretation of the passage is given by a few commentators, *e.g.* Briggs in the *Intern. Crit. Com.*, but the natural meaning seems to be as above.

[2] We have referred to this in another connexion, see p. 141. It is probable that we have in this episode a combination of an historical fact and some form of the Adonis myth.

custom is spoken of shows that it was a common one:
"Did they not sing one to another in the dances...?"
See also xxix. 5. In passing, it is worth offering an
interesting parallel to this, although the actual dancing
is not mentioned. It is given in Pausanias in reference
to the victorious Aristomenes after his defeat of the
Lacedaemonians:

When Aristomenes returned to Andania the women
threw ribbons and fresh flowers on him, and recited in
his honour a song which is sung to this day,—
To the midst of the Stenyclerian plain and to the top
    of the mountain
Aristomenes followed the Lacedaemonians[1].

In the light of these passages we may recall Judg. v. 28–
30, where the mother of Sisera is vividly depicted looking
from the "window," together with her "wise ladies," in
expectation of the return of her victorious son with the
spoils of battle. It is not an undue stretch of the
imagination to suppose that if victory instead of defeat
had fallen to Sisera's lot, we should have had a description of his mother watching the women going forth with
timbrels and dances to welcome home the victorious
warriors.

Taking these Old Testament passages by themselves,
then, there is no reason to suppose that the custom of
which they speak is anything more than a simple and
natural expression of joy and in one case, at any rate,
of thankfulness to Jahwe, for victory in battle, together
with an appropriate tribute to the victorious leader. And
the same is true in the case of other civilized peoples
of antiquity. But it is unnecessary to give illustrations

[1] Pausan. IV. xvi. 4. See, further, Hermann, *Gottesdienstliche
Alterthümer*, §§ 24, 50.

of this type of dance among them because this would throw no light on the original object of it. For this we must go to races in a lower stage of culture, among whom we are so often able to see the antecedents of both the nature and the purpose of customs which among civilized peoples appear in a developed form, and with a different purpose and meaning. If the consideration of a few examples of this type of dance among uncivilized peoples appears to lead us away somewhat from our main point, the digression must be excused on the ground that side-lights do inevitably, at times, cast their rays from a distance.

But before coming to these examples we should like to say a word about the "consecration" for battle, as it is conceivable that this may have had an indirect bearing on the "primitive" object of this type of dance. The Old Testament tells us, as we have seen, that warriors consecrated themselves before entering battle by assisting at a sacrifice[1]. The sacrifice was a means of propitiation which would induce the national God to look favourably upon the expedition and give His help to those who were about to take part in it. But this is a relatively advanced religious conception; there is a long history behind it, and some of the stages in that history are discernible in the preparation for battle among uncivilized races. We will give one instance, of many; more are unnecessary, for the same idea underlies them all. Schoolcraft, quoted by Frazer[2], tells us that

---

[1] Reference is made in 1 Sam. xxi. 5, 2 Sam. xi. 11 to an act of self-control which was also part of the consecration for battle; but this, which is found among many other races, had its special reason and does not come into consideration here.

[2] GB, *Spirits of the Corn...*, II. 145, where other examples are given.

on extraordinary occasions the bravest warriors of the
Dakotahs used to perform a dance at which they devoured the livers of dogs raw and warm in order thereby
to acquire the sagacity and bravery of the dog. The
animals were thrown to them alive, killed and cut open;
then the livers were extracted, cut into strips and hung
on a pole. Each dancer grabbed at a piece of liver with
his teeth, and chewed and swallowed it as he danced;
he might not touch it with his hands, only the medicine-
man enjoyed that privilege. Women did not join in the
dance.

To the savage this acquisition of bravery would be an
appropriate preparation for battle. In the many instances of analogous rites the choice of the animal
appears to depend upon some quality characteristic of it.
But it is possible that there is something more behind
this. In the case just cited there are two points which
suggest that the choice of the dog was not solely due to
its qualities of sagacity and bravery; the sacred dance
performed during the eating of its liver, and the prohibition to touch it, point to something sacrosanct about
the animal. Frazer points out elsewhere[1] that the
custom of killing a god in animal form

belongs to a very early stage of human culture, and is
apt in later times to be misunderstood. The advance of
thought tends to strip the old animal and plant gods of
their bestial and vegetable husk, and to leave their
human attributes (which are always the kernel of the
conception) as the final and sole residuum. In other
words, animal and plant gods tend to become purely
anthropomorphic. When they have become wholly or
nearly so, the animals and plants which were at first the
deities themselves, still retain a vague and ill-understood
connexion with the anthropomorphic gods who have

[1] *GB, Spirits of the Corn...*, i. 22.

been developed out of them. The origin of the relationship between the deity and the animal or plant having been forgotten, various stories are invented to explain it. These explanations may follow one of two lines according as they are based on the habitual or on the exceptional treatment of the sacred animal or plant. The sacred animal was habitually spared, and only exceptionally slain; and accordingly the myth might be devised to explain either why it was spared or why it was killed.

The principle here laid down is only in part applicable to the case under consideration; but it suggests that the dog, which was clearly sacred to the Dakotahs, was not eaten solely on account of its qualities of sagacity and bravery; these happened to be its characteristics which were absorbed by eating it. As a sacred animal it possessed supernatural powers, exemplified especially by its characteristic qualities. In a different stage of the development of this general conception a sacred animal would be partaken of, divine power being thereby acquired, irrespective of any quality that it might possess[1].

"Holy animals," says Robertson Smith, "and holy things generally, are primarily conceived, not as belonging to the deity, but as being themselves instinct with divine power or life. Thus a holy animal is one which has a divine life; and if it be holy to a particular god, the meaning must be that its life and his are somehow bound up together. From what is known of primitive ways of thought we may infer that this means

---

[1] The possibility is not excluded that in all cases of animals being eaten in order to absorb their qualities, their sacredness may have been the real reason at one time in the history of the rite. When this reason was forgotten and its qualities became the sole reason for eating an animal, the extension of the idea in other ways would be natural.

that the sacred animal is akin to the god, for all valid and permanent relation between individuals is conceived as kinship[1]."

In a still later stage of development, with an advanced conception of deity, a sacrifice to the god would be regarded as the means of securing what was desired, *e.g.* in the present case, divine aid to victory, as we find in 1 Sam. xiii. 9, 10.

So that it is conceivable that in an earlier stage the Semitic forbears of the Israelites partook of a sacrifice preparatory to battle in the belief that by this means the strength of the god would be imparted to them.

So much then for the question of consecration for battle. We turn now to consider the purpose of the sacred dance in connexion with battle among some of the uncivilized races.

II

As far as one can gather from the evidence there seem to be, in regard to this type of dance in its more primitive forms, two purposes which are apparently quite distinct. The first has for its object the quieting or propitiation of the ghosts of those slain in battle; in this case the dance is not the central rite, but none the less indispensable. The following is an example of this among the natives of the Indian Archipelago:

In the island of Timor, when a warlike expedition has returned in triumph bringing the heads of the vanquished foe, the leader of the expedition is forbidden by religion and custom to return at once to his own house. A special hut is prepared for him, in which he has to reside for two months, undergoing bodily and spiritual purification....That these observances are dictated by fear of

[1] *Religion of the Semites*, p. 288.

the ghosts seems certain; for from another account of the ceremonies performed on the return of a successful head-hunter in the same island we learn that the sacrifices are offered on this occasion to appease the soul of the man whose head has been taken off. The people think that some misfortune would befall the victor were such offerings omitted. Moreover, a part of the ceremony consists of a dance accompanied by a song, in which the death of the slain man is lamented and his forgiveness is entreated.

An argumentative plea, addressed to the slain man, is then pronounced in extenuation of the unfortunate necessity of his having had to lose his head[1]. It is evident that in this case the entire ceremony is an act of propitiation to the soul of the slain lest his ghost should bring some evil on the head of the slayer; the dance is, of course, performed as a cómpliment to the enraged ghost.

We take another example from a different part of the world:

Among the Roro-speaking tribes of British New Guinea homicides were secluded in the warriors' clubhouse. They had to pass the night in the building, but during the day they might paint and decorate themselves and dance in front of it....Finally, those warriors who had never killed a man before assumed a beautiful ornament made of fretted turtle shell, which none but homicides were allowed to flaunt in their head-dresses. Then came a dance, and that same night the men who wore the honourable badge of homicide for the first time were chased about the village; embers were thrown at them and firebrands waved in order, apparently, to

[1] *GB, Taboo and the Perils of the Soul*, pp. 165 f. (1911); the account is taken from S. Müller, *Reizen en Ondergoekingen in den Indischen Archipel*, II. 252 (1857). For another example see Chalmers, *op. cit.* p. 182.

drive away the souls of the dead enemies, who seemed
to be conceived as immanent in some way in the head-
gear of their slayers[1].

Here again, while the dance does not form the central
part of the ceremony, it is evidently an essential part
of it, performed in honour of the slain. The interior of
the warriors' club-house was evidently considered a
place of safety, hence the retirement into it during the
night, the time when the ghosts were most to be feared.
The dance which followed next day must be regarded
as an act of propitiation; this concerned the veterans.
The novices had their special dance, also a propitiatory
rite, while the firebrands hurled at their heads in the
evening gave the quietus to the ghosts of the men slain
by them.

Once more, among the Arunta of Central Australia it
is likewise the custom to perform a vigorous dance on
the return from battle[2]. In this case the dance com-
prises the whole ceremony, from which one can gather
the importance of it in the eyes of these people. It is
difficult to say whether the dance here is an act of propitiation or whether it serves to frighten away the ghosts
of the slain, who are supposed to follow their slayers;
probably, we should say, the former, since the frightening
away of ghosts usually takes a different form.

As a few examples of many these cases of the dance
taking place after the return from victory show that
one of its purposes was the propitiation of the ghosts
of the slain.

[1] C. G. Seligmann, *The Melanesians of British New Guinea*,
p. 298 (1910), quoted by Frazer, *Taboo and the Perils of the Soul*,
p. 168.
[2] Spencer and Gillen, *The Native Tribes of Central Australia*,
pp. 493 f. (1899).

We turn now to some other instances in which the dance had a different purpose. An old historian of Madagascar informs us that

while the men are at the wars, and until their return, the women and girls cease not day and night to dance, and neither lie down nor take food in their own homes.... They believe that by dancing they impart strength, courage, and good fortune to their husbands; accordingly during such times they give themselves no rest, and this custom they observe very religiously[1].

A similar result is believed to be brought about by dancing, according to Mr Fitzgerald Marriott, among West African tribes. He says that while the Ashantee war was raging he

saw a dance performed by women whose husbands had gone as carriers to the war. They were painted white, and wore nothing but a short petticoat. At their head was a shrivelled old sorceress in a very short white petticoat....All carried white brushes made of buffalo or horse tails, and as they danced they sang, " Our husbands have gone to Ashanteeland; may they sweep their enemies off the face of the earth[2]!"

Again, among the Thompson Indians of British Columbia, " when the men were on the war-path, the women performed dances at frequent intervals. These dances were believed to ensure the success of the expedition." The same holds good among the Yuki tribe of Indians in California; the women at home danced, believing that this would ensure victory. So, too, among the Haida women who danced and sang while their husbands were

[1] De Flacourt, *Histoire de la Grande Isle Madagascar*, pp. 97 f. (1658), quoted by Frazer, *GB, The Magic Art*, i. 131 (1911).
[2] *The Secret Tribal Societies of West Africa*, p. 17, quoted by Frazer, *op. cit.* i. 132.

away fighting; also among the women in the Kafir district of the Hindoo Koosh of whom Sir George Robertson reports that he

more than once watched the dancers dancing at midnight and in the early morning, and could see by the fitful glow of the wood-fire how haggard and tired they looked, yet how gravely and earnestly they persisted in what they regarded as a serious duty[1].

In all these cases the dancing is in the nature of sympathetic magic, and has, therefore, an entirely different purpose from that of the previous instances cited, namely that of ensuring victory. While in the cases of ghost-propitiation the dancing, though essential, is subordinate, in the sympathetic magical, or telepathic, type it is central.

One other example is worth giving, for it is one in which the dancing takes place as a welcome to the warriors on their return from battle, and is, therefore, not of a telepathic nature; on the other hand, it does not appear to be undertaken with the idea of propitiating the ghosts of the slain, while the frightening of them away is not done by the dancers. Frazer, quoting van der Roest[2], gives this example in the following words:

In Windessi, Dutch New Guinea, when a party of head-hunters has been successful, and they are nearing home, they announce their approach and success by blowing on triton shells. Their canoes are also decked with branches. The faces of the men who have taken a head are blackened with charcoal. If several have

---

[1] Frazer, *op. cit.* i. 133 f.

[2] *Uit het leven der Bevolking van Windessi*, in the "Tijdschrift voor Indische Taal-Landen Volkenkunde," XL. 157 f. (1898); *GB, Taboo and the Perils of the Soul*, pp. 169 f.

taken part in killing the same victim, his head is divided among them. They always time their arrival so as to reach home in the early morning. They come rowing to the village with a great noise, and the women stand ready to dance in the verandahs of the houses....The day is spent very quietly. Now and then they drum or blow on the conch; at other times they beat the walls of the houses with loud shouts to drive away the ghosts of the slain.

If, as seems probable, we have here a case of the dance taking place as a welcome home, and as a mark of honour to the victorious warriors, then we are justified in regarding it as the remains of the fuller form of the dance which was performed during the *whole* period of the absence of the warriors, and with a different object. In any case, such a remnant, involving a transition from one purpose to another, would be in the natural order of things,—the original purpose of the dance being an act of imitative magic to effect victory, the remnant being merely a form of welcome home to the victorious warriors; and such a transition could be paralleled by analogies, as every folklorist is well aware[1]. In course of time the original purpose or purposes of the dance would be completely forgotten, and when a reason was sought it would be simply and solely that of the welcome to the home-coming victors.

It is this latter, and this alone, which is the purpose of this type of dance in the Old Testament. But that the custom, like all ancient customs, must have a long history behind it, and that the ostensible purpose or purposes of such customs vary according to the cultural stage of the people among whom they are in vogue, will

---

[1] *E.g.* in such cases as the May-pole dance, and the dances round the Midsummer fires.

be generally allowed. We venture, therefore, to suggest the possibility that in its very much earlier phases among the ancestors of the Israelites some such objects as those indicated were connected with this type of dance.

*　　*　　*　　*

SUMMARY AND CONSIDERATIONS

Joyful expressions for victory in battle lie in the nature of things; and since dancing is, and always has been, one of the means of giving vent to this feeling, its mention in the Old Testament in this connexion is what might be expected. In the few examples of this dance recorded in the Old Testament the points to be noted are that it is performed as an act of thanksgiving to Jahwe; this stamps it as in the nature of a sacred rite. It is also a welcome home to the victorious warriors and a tribute to their bravery; but in all probability at the back of this there was always the thought of the real author of the victory, the national God; for it was in His name that the warriors had consecrated themselves for the battle, and in His name that they had, therefore, gone forth to fight (cp. Deut. xx. 1 ff.). Moreover, it has to be remembered that the nation's enemies were always regarded as the enemies of the national God. The religious character of the rite is thus emphasized. A further point is that these dances, together with accompanying music, were performed by women. As it was the men who had gone forth to fight it will be argued that there could be none but women to perform the dances. At the same time, it cannot be supposed that a district would be wholly denuded of men; some, it may reasonably be expected, remained at home for various reasons;

see *e.g.* Deut. xx. 6–8, xxiv. 5. But the performance of the rite seems to have been entirely restricted to women. It may be that there was in its early origins some reason for this, for we find a similar restriction among races of lower civilization. This type of dance is quite distinct from the war-dance; whether there was anything in the nature of a war-dance among the Israelites we have no means of ascertaining; it is never even hinted at in the Old Testament. On the other hand, there was preparation for battle in the form of sacrifice to Jahwe.

There were some other customs regarding preparation and "consecration" for battle among the Israelites which point to the lingering of very old-world conceptions; this fact offers some justification for the contention that this type of sacred dance may possibly be the remains, in a developed form, of a rite which originally contained some similar old-world conception. By "remains, in a developed form," we mean a rite shorn of its original content, but which continues to be observed, and has a new meaning assigned to it. We have in the Old Testament distinct references to the taboo on sexual intercourse for warriors previous to battle (Deut. xxiii. 10, 11; 1 Sam. xxi. 4, 5 [5, 6 in Hebr.]; 2 Sam. xi. 11).

The extension of this kind of taboo to warriors on an expedition is common among rude peoples, and we know that it had place among the Arabs, and was not wholly obsolete as late as the second century of Islām[1].

In reference to the rule laid down in Deut. xxiii. 10, 11, Frazer rightly points out that

---

[1] Robertson Smith, *The Religion of the Semites*, p. 455, where references to original authorities are given. See also Stade, *Biblische Theologie des Alten Testaments*, I. 148.

it suffices to prove that the custom of continence observed in time of war by the Israelites, as by a multitude of savage and barbarous peoples, was based on a superstitious, not a rational motive. To convince us of this it is enough to remark that the rule is often observed by warriors for some time after their victorious return, as also by the persons left at home during the absence of the fighting men. In these cases the observance of the rule evidently does not admit of a rational explanation, which could hardly, indeed, be entertained by anyone conversant with savage modes of thought[1].

There is ample evidence to show that this custom was not observed from fear of dissipating physical strength, but simply owing to the belief that any contact whatsoever with women made a man effeminate; it extended even to the touching of women's apparel. We do not maintain that the Israelites were necessarily conscious of the reason why they observed this taboo; it may or may not have been so; but what we contend is that the continued existence among them of such an old-world rite, whatever purpose was assigned for its performance, justifies belief in the possibility that the sacred dance in celebration of victory is the remains of another old-world custom and conception to which a new meaning was given. The consideration of some analogous examples of this type of dance among the uncultured races suggests that in its origin it was a magical rite performed by the women to ensure victory. This was, however, only one of the purposes of this type of dance; another object of it was the quieting or propitiating of the ghosts

---

[1] *GB, Taboo and the Perils of the Soul*, p. 158; for further examples see pp. 161 ff., and *The Magic Art*, i. 125 ff. Conceivably the taboo on the persons left at home during the absence of the fighting men may have originally had something to do with the victory dance being performed by women alone.

of those slain in battle. That it ever had this object among the Israelites or their forbears it would be rash to deny, knowing what is recorded in the Old Testament regarding the attitude of the living towards the dead[1]; but no *data* upon which to go occur in the Old Testament.

[1] See the present writer's *Immortality and the Unseen World*, chaps. VIII–X.

CHAPTER X

THE SACRED DANCE AS A MARRIAGE RITE

I

In the Old Testament there are quite a number of references to marriage[1], but there is very little about the ritual in connexion with or about the festivities which took place at weddings. The wedding feast is mentioned in Judg. xiv. 12, 17, where it is spoken of as lasting seven days; in the Apocrypha we also have mention of it in Tobit ix. 1 ff., xii. 1; according to x. 7 it lasts fourteen days. The *Chuppah, i.e.* the canopy under which the bride and bridegroom stand during the wedding-ceremony, is referred to in Ps. xix. 5 (6 in Hebr.), Joel ii. 16; cp. Tobit vii. 14, 15. The marriage procession is mentioned in 1 Macc. ix. 37 ff., in connexion with it "timbrels and minstrels" are spoken of. The only place in the Old Testament in which the ceremonial dance at a wedding is specifically referred to is in Cant. vi. 13 (vii. 1 in Hebr.); this runs, according to the R.V. rendering:

> Return, return, O Shulammite;
> Return, return, that we may look upon thee.
> Why will ye look upon the Shulammite,
> As upon the dance of Mahanaim?

The passage may be explained in this way (the justification for the interpretation will be given afterwards):

---

[1] *E.g.* Gen. xxiv. 49 ff., xxix. 27; Judg. xiv. 7; Isa. lxi. 10; Jer. ii. 32, vii. 34, xxv. 10; Ps. xlv. 10 ff.; Cant. iii. 6–11; cp. 3 Macc. iv. 8. In the New Testament we have more details, *e.g.* Matth. xxii. 2, xxv. 1 ff.; Lk. xii. 36; John ii. 1 ff.

It is the beginning of the "king's week"; the people are
gathered to witness the sword-dance of the bride; as she
is the "queen" she is spoken of as the "Shulammite"
(= "Shunammite")¹ because this was the type of a
"fair damsel" (see 1 Kings i. 3, 4; cp. Cant. i. 8, v.
9); it is an honorific title conferred on brides during their
"queenship." The people cry out to her: "Turn, turn,"
i.e. in her dance; it is a word of encouragement, they
wish also to observe all her movements. The bridegroom, who is standing by, is pleased at the favourable
reception accorded to his bride, and, in oriental fashion,
asks them why they gaze upon this fair damsel who is
dancing with a sword in her hand? They reply, as he
expects them to, with a song in praise of her beauty:
"How beautiful are thy feet in sandals..." (vii. 1 ff.),
i.e. they begin with a reference to the dance she is performing before them, to her step and other movements
of her body. The expression "dance of Maḥanaim²" is
applied to the dance because of the sword that is carried
and waved about during its performance; there is a
war-like look about it, hence the name war-dance or
"dance of hosts"; probably also the name contains a
reference to the purpose for which the dance was performed; to this we shall come in a moment.

Now there can be little doubt but that this passage
reflects the customs at weddings such as are to be seen
at the present day among the Syrian peasants who, like
the dwellers in the Arabian Desert, have preserved their
customs from time immemorial³. A most interesting

¹ See König, *Hebr. und Aram. Wörterbuch*, p. 505, and cp. the
Sept. τῇ Σουμανείτιδι (Cod. B).
² *Kimēhôlath hammaḥanaim.* Cp. the Septuagint rendering:
ὡς χοροὶ τῶν παρεμβολῶν.
³ Curtiss, *Primitive Semitic Religion To-day*, p. 52, says, "The

account of a wedding among the Syrian peasants, which throws a flood of light upon this difficult passage in *Canticles*, is recorded by Wetzstein[1]; the points which specially concern us may be briefly mentioned here. When, among these peasants, the day of a wedding is fixed the neighbours gather at the village threshing-floor where the marriage takes place. The bridegroom and bride are proclaimed king[2] and queen, and are treated as such during the seven days after the wedding, which are given up to dancing and feasting. The throne of the "royal" pair is the threshing-sledge; here they sit and watch the festivities during the "king's week," as these seven days are called. The threshing-floor is the court of the king and queen. It is in the evening of the wedding-day that the sword-dance takes place; this is performed by the bride alone before the "king" and the assembled villagers. The sword which the bride carries and brandishes during her dance is said to symbolize and proclaim the fact that she is prepared to defend herself from all unlawful approach from other suitors. This explanation is probably not the original one; for it is questionable whether among the Syrian peasants this dance was always performed by the bride. Kremer describes a marriage, for example, in the neighbourhood of Beirut, at which during the wedding procession a sword-dance took place; it was performed by two young men, friends of the

tenacity with which the Oriental mind, if left to itself, holds that which has always been, and turns to it as unerringly as the needle to the pole, has often been observed, and is our guaranty that we may find primitive religious conditions among people with whom, if we approach them in the right way, we may hold intercourse to-day." This may certainly apply to the present instance.

[1] In the *Zeitschrift für Ethnologie*, pp. 287 ff. (1873).
[2] Cp. the reference to the king in Cant. i. 4.

bridegroom; they were very lightly clad in light-blue *kumbâz* with white turban. Each held a small round shield made of hide and a sword; they fought in rhythmic time, smiting each other's shields, and moving forward the whole time with the procession[1]. Among the Bedouin Arabs again, according to Doughty[2], a sword-dance forms one of the ceremonies at weddings; here, too, it is performed by friends of the bridegroom. This is also the case among the Moslems in Palestine[3].

The object and meaning of this sword-dance, by whomsoever performed, is difficult to ascertain. It is held, and at first sight the contention seems partly justified, that we have here a relic of the very ancient custom of marriage by capture; but apart from the fact that the sword in the hand of the *bride* scarcely bears this out, grave doubts exist as to whether there ever was such a custom[4]. There are reasons for believing that this dance may originally have had a different purpose altogether. The subject is far too large and intricate to go into here, but Crawley has shown by numerous examples that certain evil influences are supposed to be

[1] *Mittel-Syrien und Damascus*, p. 123 (1853).
[2] *Arabia Deserta*, II. 118 (1921).
[3] See Rothstein's article, "Moslemische Hochzeitsgebräuche in Lifta bei Jerusalem," in Dalman's *Palästinajahrbuch*, 1910, pp. 102–123, especially 110–114; a photographic illustration of a sword-dance is given on p. 102; and Klein in the *Zeitschrift des Deutschen Palästinischen Vereins*, VI. 94 ff. (1883).
[4] "Its general unscientific nature has been demonstrated by Mr Fison and Dr Westermarck....The theory, then, that mankind in general, or even a particular section of mankind, even in normal circumstances were accustomed to obtain their wives by capture from other tribes, may be regarded as exploded. There have been, of course, and still are, sporadic cases of capture of wives from hostile tribes or others, but such cannot prove a rule." Crawley, *The Mystic Rose: A Study of Primitive Marriage*, p. 367 (1902).

abroad at the time of marriages, and that these have to be warded off by various means[1]. To give but one or two of these examples: "Amongst the Bheels and Bheelalahs the groom touches the 'marriage shed' with a sword." This, like the custom among the Bechuanas of the bridegroom throwing an arrow into the hut before he enters to take his bride, is done in order to scare away evil spirits or other harmful influences; this is also the reason, as Crawley points out, of the old Roman custom of a bridegroom combing the bride's hair with a spear, the *coelibaris hasta*. So that it is quite conceivable that the sword-dance is a relic of the custom of warding off what are supposed to be invisible foes who gather around at the time of marriages[2].

A dance of another kind, but which may also be a relic of the same custom, is mentioned by Dalman as existing among the Bedouin Arabs. When the bride comes into the house of the bridegroom she performs a dance in slow movement while holding a lighted candle in each hand with outstretched arms; she turns in all directions so as to appear like a star[3].

A few details may now be given of the dance as a marriage rite among the Jews of post-biblical times who have in innumerable ways kept up customs dating from time immemorial. We are not thinking here, any more than in the preceding examples, of the ordinary dancing at weddings which invariably took place as an expression of festive enjoyment; our concern is with ritual dances

---

[1] *Op. cit.* pp. 323 ff.

[2] For the reasons why these maleficent influences should be believed to be present on such occasions see Crawley's work, chaps. XIII, XIV.

[3] *Palestinischer Diwan*, p. 254 (1901). For the custom among the Arabs of the Hedjaz see Featherman, *op. cit.* v. 402.

which, originally at any rate, had a specific and serious object, justifying the epithet "sacred" being applied to them.

During the wedding procession through the streets it was customary for all who could do so to join in and dance in front of the bride, who is spoken of as the "queen"; this was done in her honour. Rabbi Tarphon (2nd century A.D.), we are told, on one such occasion caused the bride to be brought into his house, where she was bathed, anointed, and adorned by his mother and sister. Then he bade his pupils accompany her with songs and dances to the house of the bridegroom[1]. Rabbis of high repute danced in front of brides with myrtle-boughs in their hands. It was also part of the marriage ceremony for a dance, in which the dancers held myrtle-boughs in their hands, to be performed in front of the bridal pair[2]. The perfume of the myrtle is mystically described as dispelling the odour of hell-fire; though why there should be any danger of that odour during the marriage ceremony is not stated. Doubtless we have here an echo of the old-world conception mentioned above. We are reminded of the same thing when we read that among the Jews of Egypt in the Middle Ages during the wedding procession the bride wore a helmet, and, with a sword in her hand, led the procession with a dance[3]. It is possible that the same conception lies behind a custom noted among the Jews of Persia and elsewhere:

traces of the well-known stepping of the bride into seven circles towards the bridegroom appear in some forms of

---

[1] Krauss, *Talmudische Archäologie*, II. 39 (1911).

[2] Bacher, *Aggada der Palestinischen Amoraim*, III. 36 (1897); *JE*, VIII. 341 f.

[3] Abrahams, *Jewish Life in the Middle Ages*, p. 193 (1896).

the Jewish wedding service. The Jewish bridegroom was placed in the centre, and the bride turned round him thrice. Or the bride and bridegroom were seated side by side, and the assembled company danced round them[1].

An encircling dance had the purpose (one among others, according to circumstances) of keeping off evil influences.

A different purpose lies behind the dance performed among the Jews of the Caucasus, though the dancers are probably not conscious of it: some days before the wedding

three or four girls, relatives of the bride, put on her clothes and invite other girls to sleep in a special room with her. Toward evening the groom sends meat and rice-flour to the bride and her friends. The latter go out and sprinkle the flour on the young people who dance while the boys and girls clap their hands[2].

This, in all probability, reflects an ancient rite, in the nature of imitative magic, for the purpose of ensuring a fruitful marriage. A similar purpose may be discerned in another custom at Jewish oriental weddings, according to which the newly-married pair leapt thrice over a bowl of water in which a fish was swimming about[3].

Among the Jews of all ages, then, the sacred dance

[1] Abrahams, op. cit. pp. 195 f.; cp. with this the rite in the ancient Indian ritual, in which the bride takes seven steps towards the bridegroom; at the seventh he seizes her by the foot, Winternitz, Das altindische Hochzeitsrituell, in "Denkschriften der Kaiserlichen Akademie der Wissenschaften," xl. 51 (1892).

[2] Grunwald, in JE, viii. 346 a, quoting from Chorny, Sefer ha-Massa'ot, p. 298.

[3] Abrahams, op. cit. p. 196. For marriage rites among Jews and Mohammedans in Palestine to-day see Baldensperger in the Quarterly Statement of the Pal. Exploration Fund, 1899, pp. 140 ff., 1900, pp. 181 ff., 1901, pp. 173 ff.

as a wedding ceremony had an important place, and though its purposes may have been entirely forgotten, the rite itself continued.

II

A brief glance at some rites, analogous to those just referred to, as existing among some other peoples will not be without interest. The idea of "royalty" attaching to the bridal pair is seen in Morocco at the present day; the bridegroom is looked upon and treated as a sultan, and his bachelor friends act as his ministers (*wazara*)[1]. Among the Malays the bride and bridegroom are called *Raja sari*, "the sovereigns of the day," and "it is a polite fiction that no command of their's, during their one day of sovereignty, may be disobeyed[2]." Many similar examples could be given; the underlying idea is that by a change of identity[3],—that it is purely fictitious is no matter—the dangers which are conceived of, however vaguely, as attending those about to be joined in marriage, are mitigated. Westermarck says:

A very large number of marriage ceremonies spring from the feeling or idea that bride and bridegroom are in a state of danger, and therefore stand in need of purification and of special protection against magical influences and evil spirits;

in this class of customs he includes dancing[4]. *Why* dancing should be supposed to have this effect is another question to which, presumably, different answers will be given. For our own part, we are inclined to believe that at the bottom of it lies a connexion with the original

[1] Westermarck, *Marriage Ceremonies in Morocco*, p. 144 (1914).
[2] Skeat, *Malay Magic*, p. 388 (1910).
[3] On this, see further Crawley, *op. cit.* pp. 327 ff., 335 ff.
[4] *Op. cit.* p. 321.

idea and purpose of the sacred dance, viz. the imitation, and therefore the pleasing, of supernatural powers, as already pointed out (see p. 22); not that there was necessarily any consciousness of this; but from the earliest times dancing had had this purpose, and the custom continued without a reason for it being assigned. Not but what the rite as a marriage ceremony may, and doubtless did, have other purposes as well; but these may either have been superimposed, or what is quite possible, a different train of ideas gave rise to them. But behind them all lay, in the first instance, this propitiatory act performed in honour of some supernatural power. All festive dancing at weddings may be regarded as having originated from this. To quote Westermarck again:

> Ceremonies which once had a purpose may, in course of time, become entirely meaningless, and yet continue to be practised; and ceremonies may also be direct expressions of emotional states, whether combined with a special purpose or not. Just as funeral rites and mourning observances, even when they are intended to protect the survivors against the dead man's ghost or the contagion of death, are very largely similar to or identical with natural expressions of sorrow or grief, so the precautions taken at a wedding assume the shape of joyful performances, such as dancing, music, singing...[1].

Among these ceremonies which have become entirely meaningless, but are continued as a joyful or picturesque performance, was the sword-dance referred to in the Old Testament. This, as we have already noticed, is in all probability the relic of a rite which had the purpose of averting evil influences; it was a more aggressive means

---

[1] *Op. cit.* p. 344.

of combating these, the change of identity being a passive form serving the same purpose. But as the sword-dance had this combative purpose, any other weapon might have been equally efficacious; indeed, if, as we have reason to suppose, the sword-dance is but the latest form of a very ancient rite, we should expect to find that in its more primitive forms other weapons would be employed, for the sword was, comparatively speaking, a modern weapon. So that while, on the one hand, *e.g.* among the Druses of Syria, the sword-dance figures as a necessary rite at weddings[1], and among the Moroccans the bridegroom carries a sword as long as the marriage ceremonies continue[2], we find that in the ancient Indian ritual the bride when formally presented to the bridegroom at the wedding ceremony places a whip or an arrow in his hand[3]. That in some cases the carrying or presenting the weapon is unaccompanied by the dance need cause no surprise; they are but exceptions to the general rule, and it is made up for afterwards. An echo of the primitive rite is doubtless to be discerned among the Malayans; at a royal wedding a performance is given by dancing girls and fencers[4]; and at ordinary weddings during the marriage procession there is dancing and fencing to the accompaniment of music and singing[5].

There are various other wedding ceremonies, some accompanied by dancing and some not, which originally had, and often still have, the purpose of counteracting malign influences at the time of marriage; these in-

---

[1] Featherman, *Social History of the Races of Mankind*, v. 480 (1881).
[2] Westermarck, *op. cit.* p. 251.
[3] Winternitz, *Das altindische Hochzeitsrituell*, XL. 30.
[4] Skeat, *Malay Magic*, p. 374.   [5] Skeat, *op. cit.* p. 381.

fluences are, or rather were, partly due to the belief in mysterious, vaguely-conceived dangers which the sexes reciprocally ascribed to each other[1], and partly to the strangeness of feeling generated by the knowledge that a new state of life was about to be entered upon which would bring about new experiences as regards oneself, and new relationships as regarded others. As to the former; it is very likely that the "Henna-dance," which always takes place at weddings among the Malays, had the original purpose of counteracting the dangers alluded to, e.g., the evil eye, possibly; this dance takes its name from the ceremony of dabbing henna on the centre of the palm of the bride. Skeat, in describing the dance, says:

A picturesque feature of it is a small cake of henna, which is contained in a brazen cup and surrounded by candles. This cup is carried by the dancer who has to keep turning it over and over without letting the candles be extinguished by the wind arising from the rapid motion.

The step is called the "Henna-dance step," and the tune accompanying it is called the "Henna-staining tune[2]." Doubtless this is an elaboration of the original form of the dance, and a further purpose has been superimposed —the turning of the cup without extinguishing the candles may be differently explained, though it must

[1] "For practical purposes, as is hardly necessary to premise, the complex fears of men and women are often subconscious, or are only expressed as a feeling of diffidence with regard to the novel proceedings, and also are not always focussed on the personality of either party with its inherent dangerous properties nor stimulated by conscious realisation of particular dangers.... We have, however, seen cases where the individual in marriage is consciously aware that it is his human partner who is to be feared" (Crawley, op. cit. p. 323).

[2] Skeat, op. cit. p. 377, and for other dances at weddings see pp. 388 f., 392.

be a magical rite of some kind—but the henna on the palms certainly seems to point to a means of averting the evil eye.

As to the fears at entering upon a new state, we may be pardoned for quoting Westermarck once more, for he is our foremost authority on the whole subject. He writes:

A marriage implies not only that the parties enter into new relations to each other's people, but very frequently that one of them, through the change of domicile, is actually transferred to the other one's family group. And it implies other changes in the social grouping of people: either party passes from one social class into another, the bridegroom from the class of the bachelors to that of the married men, the bride from the class of the girls to that of the married women. This re-grouping also finds expression in the marriage ritual, as when the hair of the bride is arranged in the fashion of married women, or she ceremonially assumes the head-dress worn by them, or when the bride dances first with the unmarried girls and then with the married women, and the bridegroom first with the bachelors and then with the married men[1].

Here the dance is clearly in the nature of an initiatory ceremony into one class from another, and it has the effect of familiarizing each party with the new status and condition; it may, therefore, be regarded as serving a kind of prophylactic purpose.

This has taken us some way from the sword-dance; but it all really arises from this; for all that has been said points to the belief in the existence of undefined dangers in marriage, and the means to counteract these; and numberless other examples are available. But our

---

[1] *The History of Human Marriage*, ii. 584 (1921); see also Featherman, *op. cit.* i. 208.

main point here is to show how frequently, for whatever reasons, the dance has a part to play in the rites performed.

III

We take now a brief glance at one or two other wedding ceremonies in which the dance figures prominently. We have seen that at Harvest Festivals dances were performed by some peoples for the purpose of making the crops grow. Either by leaping high during the dance, or by the dancers personating the spirits of fertility, or by dances of other kinds, it was believed that the desired effect could be produced. Two ideas often coalesce in such dances: that of a propitiatory act in honour of the god of fertility, and that of an act of imitative magic; but, of course, the two are not always or necessarily combined in the same dance. The purpose of this type of dance, however, is not confined to that of ensuring good crops. We are told, for example, that among the Mandan Indians on the occasion of their great annual festival, a man acts the part of a buffalo bull in the buffalo dance, "the object of which was to ensure a plentiful supply of buffaloes during the ensuing year[1]." To the same circle of ideas belongs that according to which a plentiful supply of fish can be procured by dancing[2]. Instances need not be multiplied. It is evident that the belief was, and probably still is, widespread of dancing being the means of ensuring fertility. Now if this was so in regard to crops and animals, may it not be possible that the same belief existed in regard to human beings? Even though the purpose might have

[1] Frazer, *GB*, *The Scapegoat*, p. 171.
[2] Frazer, *GB*, *The Spirits of the Corn and of the Wild*, II. 255.

been entirely forgotten the practice might still be continued. It is conceivable that this idea, though forgotten, may underlie the ceremony of "the cleaning of the wheat" to be used at the wedding feast among the Moroccans; this is performed by married women and girls; while some of them are cleaning the wheat others dance and sing, keeping time by clapping their hands; it is so necessary that the dancing should continue during the whole ceremony that when the dancers get tired others take their place[1]. Among the same people the *wazara* (see p. 184) perform a ceremonial dance in the house of the bride[2]. This may also have been the original purpose of the *epithalamium* among the Greeks, sung after the wedding feast in the evening before the door of the bridal chamber by a chorus of maidens who danced while they sang; Theocritus refers to this in his eighteenth Idyll ("The Epithalamium of Helen"):

> And so in Sparta long ago the maids
> With blooming hyacinths their locks among,
> Within the halls of fair-haired Menelaus
> Before the newly-limnèd bride chamber
> Their dances set—twelve girls, the city's pride,
> The flower of Lacedemon's maids,—what time
> The younger son of Atreus wooed and won
> Helen, the darling child of Tyndareus,
> And took her to his bower. In one accord
> They sang, with measured beat and woven steps,
> While loud the halls rang with the marriage-lay[3].

Other instances of a similar character could easily be adduced. The idea is not so fantastic as, at first sight,

---

[1] Westermarck, *Marriage Ceremonies in Morocco*, p. 90.
[2] Westermarck, *op. cit.* p. 144.
[3] H. A. Metcalf's translation, *The Idylls and Epigrams of Theocritus...* (1905).

it may appear to some. When we are dealing with things from the point of view of uncultured man we must not look for the laws of cause and effect to follow the course which would appeal to us. He believes that he can put into motion the working of Nature by means of his own devising; and if he induce or assist the spirits of fertility in producing corn and buffaloes, there is no reason why he should not by the same means assist them in quickening the child-bearing capacity of a woman.

Many other examples could be given of the dance as a marriage rite, but we must content ourselves with the few following references to it among peoples in very different parts of the world:

The Indians of British Columbia, Westermarck, *The History of Human Marriage*, I. 458 f.; the natives of Central Africa, Miss Alice Werner, *The Natives of British Central Africa*, p. 131 (1906); the Kayans of Borneo, H. Ling Roth, *The Natives of Sarawak and North Borneo*, I. 114 f. (1896); the aborigines of Australia, Howitt, *The Native Tribes of South Eastern Australia*, pp. 233 f., 245 (1904); the natives of Tahiti, Featherman, *op. cit.* II. 33 f.; the natives of New Britain, George Brown, *Melanesians and Polynesians*, p. 116 (1910).

* * * *

SUMMARY AND CONSIDERATIONS

Once only in the Old Testament is there mention of a ceremonial wedding dance, though there are frequent references to other marriage customs. We have to look in other directions for the meaning and purpose of this type of sacred dance. From the custom among the Bedouin Arabs it seems that at their weddings the sword-dance forms one of the most important ceremonies; and from this we may gather that the "dance of Mahanaim," mentioned in Canticles, was a similar sword-dance. Various considerations point to the probability of this sword-dance being a relic of the custom of warding off what were conceived to be malign influences at the times of weddings. Traces of the same old-world idea, though, of course, entirely forgotten, are to be discerned in some of the customs among the Jews of the Middle Ages. It is possible that among them certain other ceremonies which were performed on these occasions had the object of ensuring a fruitful marriage.

Very widely spread is the custom of calling the bridegroom and the bride "king" and "queen," and of treating them as a royal pair during the whole period of the wedding festivities. The reason for this was originally that, by means of change of identity, the bridal pair might avoid the mysterious dangers which were supposed to be present. The idea presumably was that a disguise puzzled the malign visitors so that they did not know on whom to vent their spleen. It is evident that a similar purpose was served by the custom of substituting a mock bride for the real one, or of bride and bridegroom being attended by one or more persons dressed up to resemble her or him; Crawley gives interesting illustrations of both customs[1].

Some other dances in connexion with the marriage ceremony are considered; they have either the purpose of counteracting the evil influences already referred to; or else, as there are some reasons for believing, they were supposed to ensure a fruitful marriage.

[1] *The Mystic Rose*, pp. 337 ff.

It is not to be expected that we should find any trace of these purposes in the Old Testament; but the analogy of Bedouin Arab custom and that of the Jews at later periods offers presumptive evidence that the customs existed among the Israelites, though their original purpose was entirely forgotten.

CHAPTER XI

DANCING AS A MOURNING AND BURIAL RITE

I

THERE is no instance to be found in the Old Testament of dancing being performed as a mourning or burial rite; that must be acknowledged; yet in spite of this there are strong reasons for believing that the custom did exist among the Israelites. The silence does not imply that the rite was not in vogue; there are, also, sufficient reasons to account for the absence of reference to it. In the first place, excepting incidentally we should not necessarily expect it to be mentioned at all; it was not a public rite; if it had been one might conceivably have looked for some reference to it in the records, supposing it to have been performed on some great or special occasion; but as a private rite there was no reason for its being recorded in Hebrew literature. Another reason for its not being mentioned is because its original significance and importance had, it may be confidently asserted, been forgotten; like some other mourning and burial customs it would have been kept up for no other reason than that it had been handed down from time immemorial; so that there was no point in speaking of it. Moreover, in the case of some other Israelite mourning customs there is only here and there incidental mention in the Old Testament, although some of them were certainly very often practised, *e.g.* flute-playing, laceration of the body (modified later by the rending of the

garment), cutting off of the hair, baring the feet, covering
the head, the funeral feast; it might easily have happened
in the case of any one of these that the incidental
mention had not occurred (as, indeed, is the case with
flute-playing); but that silence would not have justified
denial of its existence, provided always that there were
reasons for believing that it was practised. Now, as we
shall see, in the case of dancing as a mourning or burial
rite there are reasons for believing that it was in vogue
among the Israelites, and that therefore the silence of
the Old Testament is not in itself sufficient reason for
denying that it existed among them.

There is a further potent reason for this custom never
being mentioned: its practice was incompatible with
Jahwe-worship, because of its connexion with Ancestor-
worship, and therefore the suppression (supposing it had
been mentioned) of all reference to it would have been
regarded as a sacred duty by the later redactors of the
sacred text. As is well known, the Old Testament literature was subjected to such redactions in times when a full
development in the direction of a more rigid insistence
upon and a more emphatic declaration of monotheistic
worship had taken place; under these circumstances it
would have been the most natural thing in the world
for any reference to this rite in the sacred literature to
have been deleted. So that, on this ground, again, the
silence in the Old Testament regarding this mourning
rite is no reason for denying that it existed.

But there are, on the other hand, positive grounds for
the belief that it was in existence among the Israelites:

If analogies count for anything (and in the case of
ancient customs, and especially burial rites, they are of
the greatest importance), then the fact that dancing as

a mourning or burial rite either is, or has been, widespread among all kinds of peoples all over the world would suggest that the Israelites practised it too. There are a number of other mourning and burial rites common to the races of antiquity (including the Israelites) and to the uncultured races of the present day[1]; if dancing formed an exception to these, being practised by all excepting the Israelites, there would have to be some very special reason assigned for this; but it is evident that such reason is not forthcoming.

Another reason which suggests the probability of dancing as a mourning rite among the Israelites is that it was a natural concomitant to flute-playing, which, as we know from the New Testament, was a very usual mourning rite; the two belong together, and where the one was in vogue it is reasonable to suppose that the other was not wanting. This applies, of course, to early times; it is always possible that with the development of religious ideas an antique custom may be modified, or even fall into disuse; in the present case neither the dancing nor the flute-playing fell into disuse until well into the Christian era (indeed, the former is still performed), but a modification of the custom took place in so far that they were not necessarily performed at the same time.

Then we have this further reason: it will be seen, when we come to consider the *objects* of dancing as a mourning rite, that they involve beliefs which seem to be common to man during some stages in his cultural and religious development. It is difficult to suppose that

[1] For these, see the present writer's book, *Immortality and the Unseen World: a Study in Old Testament Religion*, pp. 141 ff. (1921).

what had been characteristic of man generally should not have been so in the case of the Israelites. We touch upon this point again later.

But, finally, the strongest reason for believing that this custom was in vogue among the ancient Israelites is that it exists at the present day. Such things as mourning and burial customs are never innovations; modifications may arise, as we have just said; a custom may fall into disuse and be discontinued altogether; but when a rite is practised at the present day, it is not a new thing, but has a long history behind it. Regarding the particular example to be given presently it is known to go back at any rate to the beginning of the Christian era; but it is safe to say that it must be vastly older than that in reality; for of all customs none are so tenacious as those which have to do with mourning and burial, for they touch men at a very sensitive spot. If at *any* time such a custom as we are thinking of is known to have existed, or to exist now, it may be taken for granted that, as a matter of fact, it goes back to very much earlier, indeed to pre-historic, times. That much may be safely gathered from what we know of the customs of savage man and the way in which so many of them are still existent in modified forms. So that since, at the least, something corresponding to the sacred dance as a mourning rite is still in vogue among some of the Jews, it is hardly too much to say that that *ipso facto* proves its existence among their Hebrew ancestors in days gone by.

One other consideration may be urged. It must be allowed that the number of words found in the Old Testament for dancing is significant. When we know that dancing on various religious occasions formed an important element, as shown in the preceding chapters, the presumption is strong that it occurred also during the very solemn period of mourning.

It may, then, be contended that the cumulative effect of these arguments justifies the belief that the sacred dance as a mourning or burial rite was well known to, and practised by, the ancient Israelites, and that the silence of the Old Testament upon the subject is no reason to doubt this.

II

Among the Jews (both Ashkenazic and Sephardic) the sacred dance as a burial rite is known to have been in existence during the Christian era. During the Talmudic period (*i.e.* A.D. 500 and following centuries) it was customary, and is still, on occasion, for a laudatory speech to be made in the case of men either at the burial or afterwards. Such speeches were accompanied by what must be regarded as the remnant of some form of dance; while they were being delivered the mourners kept up a monotonous, but rhythmical, stamping of the feet; this was not applause, being too regular and incessant; it must be regarded as a means of giving vent to the emotions, just as the dance in the ordinary sense was. Its origin may have been, judging from parallels among other peoples, a sacred dance in honour of the deceased, which in course of time took this stereotyped and mechanical form. The word used is *raqa'* which occurs also in the Old Testament for the stamping of feet (2 Sam. xxii. 43, Ezek. vi. 11), though in neither case is there the slightest suggestion of dancing; but, as we have said, it is only to be regarded as a remnant of the earlier custom, not in itself a dance. The fact that it was done collectively by the mourners is a point of significance, for from what we know of funeral dances among other peoples such collective action was usual. Not but that individuals expressed their emotions in their own way, too; for we read, for example, of mourners being often carried away by the intensity of their feelings and acting in an extravagant way, tearing off their sandals and beating themselves with them; women were known during a funeral procession to jump on to the coffin. Compared with such things a dance in honour of a respected relative deceased would be a decorous proceeding. And when we remember that dancing was performed as an act of honour to the deity, a similar means of showing respect to a greatly loved and honoured person at his funeral is not so out of the question as it might seem at first. Krauss says that at funerals, in all probability, both men and women performed dances fitting to the occasion; and they certainly gesticulated with hands and fingers. He gives a concrete instance of a woman dancing before the picture of her dead son; "a proceeding not unheard of during funeral processions[1]"; the word used is *rāqad*, on which see above, p. 46.

Again, the Sephardic Jews (*i.e.* Spanish and Portuguese) have retained some ancient elements in their worship and ritual which have disappeared among the Ashkenazim, who include the bulk of the Jews. A notable instance of this is the procession round the corpse at burials. Circumambulation, a processional march round an object, cannot in its origin be distinguished from the encircling dance, for in many cases the purpose

---

[1] *Talmudische Archäologie*, II. 67 f., 483 (1911); cp. also Thomson, *The Land and the Book*: Lebanon, Damascus, and beyond Jordan, pp. 401 ff. (1886).

of the rite is the same. Nor can it be doubted that all such circumambulations are modifications of earlier forms, in which the less restrained emotions of men in an earlier and lower stage of civilization required the more exuberant outlet afforded by a dance-step of the more literal kind. It is said that "dancing and procession are sometimes confused terminologically, a result partly due to the existence of processional dances, or the enlivening of a procession by the dance[1]"; but whatever may be the case terminologically, there can be no confusion between the two essentially, for they present two modes of emotional expression, comparable with the ordinary religious dance and the ecstatic dance. Therefore there is justification for regarding the Sephardic processions round the corpse at funerals as the modification or remnant of a ceremony which was originally performed in a less controlled manner. The original meaning of the rite has of couse been forgotten long since; but, as so often happens, the rite itself, or some modification of it, is still kept up.

It is the custom at the burial of Sephardic Jews for the mourners to make seven circuits round the bier during which seven short supplications are chanted or monotoned, each supplication concluding with the words: "And continually may he walk in the land of life, and may his soul rest in the bond of life[2]." It is interesting

[1] Crawley, in *ERE*, x. 358 *a*.

[2] The mystic number, seven, in connexion with the rite will not escape notice. The whole service will be found in Gaster's *Daily and Occasional Prayers*, vol. i. (1901). The supplications, though not in precisely the same form in which they now appear, are known to go back to pre-Christian times; the antiquity of the ritual by which they are accompanied, especially when its nature is considered, will obviously be at least as great, let alone the long history behind it.

to note that this Sephardic rite can be paralleled by
something similar among other peoples. Its purpose will
be considered later.

The custom seems to have been well-known as early
as the time of Homer; in the *Iliad* (xxiii. 13) the circumambulation round the corpse of Patroclus is described.
Again, we read that five hundred disciples went in procession round the funeral pyre of Buddha, in consequence
of which the pyre kindled spontaneously[1]. D'Alviella
refers to the Latin poet Statius's description of the
funeral rites celebrated in honour of the son of Lycurgus;
among these was included a threefold procession round
the funeral pyre[2].

When the Argonauts in the poem of Apollonius
Rhodius buried their dead comrade Mopsus, they
marched round him thrice in their warrior-gear. So
among the populations of India which practise crema-
tion, the son or other relative who lights the pyre walks
thrice round it. The custom of walking round the corpse,
or the grave, after burial, is recorded of peoples as far
apart in space and culture as the Central Eskimo, the
Russian Tapps, the Buriats, the Shans, and the
Arāwaks of British Guiana[3].

At Chinese burials, after the body has been placed in
the tomb, the mourners join hands and perform a sort
of merry-go-round about the tomb; they repeat this
three days later[4]. The Irish, even at the present day,
when burying their dead, move in procession, sometimes
three times, but at least once, round the grave-yard,
accompanying the coffin[5]. This must, in all probability,

---

[1] *Sacred Books of the East*, xi. 129 (1879–1910).
[2] In *ERE*, iii. 658 b.
[3] Hartland, in *ERE*, iv. 426 b.
[4] Walse, in *ERE*, iv. 453 b.
[5] Joyce, *Social History of Ancient Ireland*, i. 301 (1903).

be a modification of an earlier form of the rite in which
the mourners went round the coffin itself; unless this be
regarded as a continuation of the funeral procession
itself; but, generally speaking, the particular custom of
which we are thinking is quite distinct from the funeral
procession.

From these instances of a modification of the sacred
dance as a mourning rite we turn now to some in which
the dancing is performed in the more literal sense.

III

Among the Arabs at the present day, and doubtless
the rite in one form or another goes back to times of
antiquity, the women and the young girls, when on their
way to the place of mourning, make two circles by
holding hands and dance what is called the *Raḳṣa* dance;
while dancing they sing:

The Almighty, the Almighty, gives and takes;
The path to the place of mourning I desire not for
  myself...[1].

Although other instances among the Arabs exist, they
are not numerous. But as to other Semitic peoples we
have been unable to discover examples.

On the other hand, there is a considerable amount of
evidence regarding its existence among the Egyptians,
both ancient and modern. In respect of the former this
occurs mainly on inscriptions, so that it is graphic as
well as informing. On one of these there is a representation of the ceremony of mourning in the chamber of
the dead; harp-players, singers, and dancers appear as
taking part in the ceremonies[2].

---

[1] Alois Musil, *Arabia Petraea*, iii. 203 (1908).
[2] For illustrations of this kind see, *e.g.*, Rosellini, *Les Monuments de l'Égypte et de la Nubie*, Pl. cxiv. fig. 2, Pl. cxvi. fig. 6

"The sculptures and paintings of the xviii–xx dynasties," says Flinders Petrie[1], "show many scenes of funeral dances; usually one woman held a tambourine aloft and beat out a rhythm on it, while others danced round. Exactly this dance may be seen now when parties of women go up to the cemeteries a fortnight or a month after a funeral; an old negress is often the drummer, and the party stop every few hundred yards along the road for a dance."

At the "Feast of Eternity" dancing always took place in honour of the dead; dancing men headed the procession in which the statue of the departed was borne. The step was rhythmic and slow, the arms being raised over the head during the dancing and the inside of the hands being turned upwards. Another position was that of stretching the right arm slantingwise upwards while the left arm was placed on the back. Behind the men three or four women follow, singing[2].

In an inscription on a tomb at Benihassan there is a representation of dances at the funeral festival of the monarch Chnomhôtep, of the period of the twelfth dynasty; the dancing is performed by women very slightly clad. Funeral processions were always accompanied by women dancing and singing[3]. In a grave near the royal tombs of Abydos, belonging to the first dynasty (before 5000 B.C.) Flinders Petrie found a curved wand, ending in a ram's horn, used for beating time in dancing[4]. There can be little doubt that this was used during the performance of the funeral dance.

(1831); Lepsius, *Denkmäler aus Aegypten und Aethiopien*, Div. II, Pls. 52, 53 (1849); Perrot et Chipiez, *Histoire de l'art dans l'antiquité : l'Égypte*, p. 701 (1882).
[1] In *ERE*, v. 238 a.   [2] Erman, *Aegypten...*, i. 336.
[3] Erman, *op. cit.* i. 338, ii. 434.
[4] Reported in the *Times*, 29th June, 1922.

As already pointed out, this rite is still to be seen among the modern Egyptians. Lane gives the following interesting description of it:

It is customary among the peasants of Upper Egypt for the female relations and friends of a person deceased to meet together by his house on each of the first three days after the funeral, and there to perform a lamentation and a strange kind of dance. They daub their faces and bosoms, and part of their dress, with mud; and tie a rope-girdle, generally made of the coarse grass called "halfa," round the waist[1]. Each flourishes in her hand a palm-stick, or a *nebboot* (a long staff), or a spear, or a drawn sword, and dances with a slow movement, and in an irregular manner, generally pacing about, and raising and depressing the body. This dance is continued for an hour or more, and is performed twice or three times in the course of the day. After the third day the women visit the tomb, and place upon it their rope-girdles; and usually a lamb, or a goat, is slain there, as an expiatory sacrifice, and a feast is made on this occasion[2].

Whether the performers of this dance know the purpose and meaning of it or not now is not stated; but there can be little doubt, knowing what we do of the object of similar dances on similar occasions among other peoples, that it had originally a twofold purpose, though these have now been amalgamated in one rite. In the first place, it was performed as an act of honour to the departed; this would have been more appropriately done on the occasion of offering the sacrifice at the tomb; probably at one time this was the procedure. But it had the further object of combating the evil spirits which

[1] Cp. Herodotus, II. 85.
[2] *An Account of the Manners and Customs of the Modern Egyptians*, II. 272 (1871).

were usually supposed to gather in the vicinity of a corpse, hence the palm-stick, etc.; this would be done on behalf of the spirit of the departed as well as of the mourners; the daubing of mud on faces and bosoms was by way of protection against the evil spirits, for it acted as a disguise. There are cases on record in which it is the angry spirit of the deceased himself who is feared and against whom protective measures are taken; but in the example before us the fact that a lamentation is made rather points to the spirit of the deceased not being feared.

This custom among the modern Moslems of Egypt may be supplemented by one or two examples of something similar among some heathen inhabitants of another part of Egypt. In writing about the Lattuka tribe of negroes in the Egyptian Soudan Frobenius says that dances are performed in honour of the dead, and he gives Baker's description of this mourning rite. The dancers are decorated in the most extraordinary manner, doubtless as a special mark of respect for the departed. About a dozen enormous ostrich feathers were stuck into the head-dress of each dancer; hanging down from the shoulder was either the skin of a leopard, or of a monkey; around the loins of every dancer was a broad piece of leather which concealed a large bell attached to the waist; these bells sounded during the dancing. Further, each dancer had the horn of an antelope hanging down from his neck, and whenever a high pitch of excitement was reached these horns were blown, whereby a sound was produced which might be described as a combination of the " hee-haw " of a donkey and the hooting of an owl. This was diversified every now and then by a circle-dance in which the women joined in with the men;

this part of the performance was done by the whole
company following a leader; it is described as a "Hell-
gallop." The women, who otherwise danced separated
from the men, were led by one of their number who was
exceedingly fat; but in spite of this physical handicap
the brave old lady persevered in the dance right to the
end. Children also took part in the rite[1].

The same custom, though differently carried out, is
in vogue among the Makaraká tribe who also belong to
the Egyptian Soudan. Ceremonial dances are performed
round their slain enemies by the Dinka tribe, inhabiting
the same country.

In the case of the Lattuka tribe it is clear that the
rite had again a dual purpose; they dressed themselves
and danced in honour of the deceased, while the bell-
ringing and horn-blowing would have effectively scared
away the evil spirits; the more excited part of the dance
may also well have been a means of frightening away
unwelcome visitors from the spirit-world.

The dance of the Dinkas round their slain enemies may
have one of two objects. Such dances are undoubtedly
at times intended to be a coaxing of the slain not to be
angry at having been killed; the dance is meant to soothe
them because it is done in their honour, and therefore
their spirits, it is thought, will not harm the slayers.
On the other hand, an encircling dance of this kind
round enemies may have the purpose of preventing the
spirits of the slain from getting abroad; the magic circle
keeps them in, and thus harm is averted.

[1] *Op. cit.* pp. 344, 408 f., 452.

IV

The religious dance among the Greeks and Romans played, as we have seen, a very important part. We should, therefore, naturally expect to find it figuring also among customs connected with mourning and burial. And there is clear evidence that this was the case[1]. Among them dancing as a mourning or burial rite was included in funeral processions and funeral games[2]. All three, dancing, processions, and games, belong together. But it was during the funeral feast, which formed the conclusion to the mourning ceremonies, that the dance figured most prominently. Illustrations of this dance as a mourning rite are given in Daremberg and Saglio, II. 848, 1385, who write thus:

Ces repas funèbres étaient accompagnés de danse. Il semble même que ces danses étaient quelquefois exécutées à part, avec plus de solennité et par un personnel plus nombreux. Dans la *Grotta del Trichinio* à Corneto elles se déroulent sur deux parois entières de la tombe; la scène se passe en plein air, sous les arbres où voltigent des oiseaux; dix danseurs s'y démènent en cadence; les hommes alternant aves les femmes, quelques-uns jouant de la lyre, de la flûte, ou des castagnettes. Parfois même

[1] Among the Romans, during the earliest periods, funerals always took place at night; for the evidence see Marquardt, *Das Privatleben der Römer*, pp. 343 f. (1886).

[2] As to funeral games see Daremberg et Saglio, *Dictionnaire des antiquités Greques et Romaines*, II. 1376 (1896...): "La présence de nombreux chars sur les vases peints du Dipylon fait croire qu'on continua à célébrer des jeux funèbres en l'honneur du mort, et cet usage persista longtemps encore, comme semble l'indiquer une peinture où un char de course est représenté à côté d'une stèle qu'on achève de décorer." Cp. Rohde, *Psyche...*, I. 224 f. As Hartland points out (*ERE*, IV. 437 *a*), "funeral games, familiar to us in classical literature, are of very wide distribution. They cannot be separated from dances, for there is no hard and fast line between the two."

ces danses donnaient bien à des concours; sur un bas-relief de Chiusi on voit, à droite, un groupe de pyrrhi-chistes et un musicien jouant de la double flûte; à gauche les juges sur une estrade[1].

The ancient Roman funeral procession was accompanied by musicians, singers, dancers and pantomimists[2]. Among funeral processions that of the ancient Roman *nobiles* is remarkable. The dead man was accompanied by all his ancestors, represented by persons resembling them in form and stature and wearing wax portrait masks (*imagines*)[3].

These *imagines maiorum* stood in the *alae* of the *atrium* of the houses of Roman nobles; they were brought out and carried in the funeral procession. The origin of this strange custom has been explained by O. Benndorf. Just as, according to antique belief, the dead lived on in the grave, which was, therefore, made into a kind of dwelling-place for them, so, it was believed, that by producing the likenesses of those who inhabited this dwelling-place, it was possible to keep in touch with their personalities[4]. Hence the setting-up of the *imagines* in the *atrium*. When they were brought out to accompany the recently departed in the funeral procession, it meant that his ancestors were actually following his body. The descriptions which have come down to us are in reference to public funerals, or those of the wealthier classes who could afford to pay for

---

[1] See also Rohde, *Psyche*..., I. 221.

[2] In Dionys. VII. 72 there is a description of such a procession in which troops danced in the dress of Sileni and Satyrs. Suet. *Caes.* 84 (Marquardt, *Das Privatleben der Römer*, pp. 352 f.).

[3] Crawley, in *ERE*, x. 356 a.

[4] *Antike Gesichtshelme und Sepulcralmasken*, p. 4 (1878), referred to by Marquardt, *Privatleben der Römer*, p. 241, and see further, pp. 353 ff.

sumptuous burials of an ostentatious character; but there is reason to believe that among the less well-to-do the same rites, though on a far more modest scale, were observed; for it has been rightly remarked that

all periods of the history of Roman burial are unified by the belief in the continued existence of the dead, and in his ghostly participation in the life of the family and the community, and by the consequent scrupulous care about proper burial, and the maintenance of right relations with the spirits of dead ancestors. The quick and the dead of ancient Rome were in a more than usually intimate communion[1].

The sacred dance, as a mark of honour to the deceased, is therefore not likely to have been neglected among the poor any more than among the rich.

V

We come now to consider some examples of dancing as a mourning or burial rite among some of the savage and semi-civilized peoples. What will strike us here as strange are the contradictory ideas regarding the purpose of the rite; but it is just these opposing ideas that will be found to be so instructive. Various customs in existence at the present day among civilized peoples are explained in the light of the ideas and practices now to be considered.

There is no doubt that the object of this rite among uncivilized races which is most common now is the honouring of the departed; but it is probably true to say that this represents the latest development regarding its purpose, and that the other reasons for which it was

[1] Showerman in *ERE*, iv. 505 *b*, 507 *b*. Cp. Daremberg et Saglio, *op. cit.* s.v. *Funus*.

performed take us back to earlier stages of the growth of savage thought regarding the departed.

We will begin by offering examples of this most developed idea and purpose of the rite.

In writing of the Kol tribes of Chota Nagpur who are remarkable for their pathetic reverence for their dead, Tylor says:

When a Ho or Munda has been burned on the funeral pile, collected morsels of his bones are carried in procession with a solemn, ghostly, sliding step, keeping time to the deep-sounding drum, and when the old woman who carries the bones in her bamboo tray lowers it from time to time, then girls who carry pitchers and brass vessels mournfully reverse them to show that they are empty; thus the remains are taken to visit every house in the village, and every dwelling of a friend or a relative for miles, and the inmates come out to mourn and praise the goodness of the departed. The bones are carried to all the dead man's favourite haunts, to the fields he cultivated, to the grave he planted, to the threshing-floor where he worked, to the village dance-room were he made merry. At last they are taken to the grave, and buried in an earthen vase upon a store of food...[1].

It is clear that the departed spirit is believed in some way to remain in the vicinity of the bones, or possibly to be inside them; and this reminds one of the quaint belief of life residing in the bones which occurs in the Old Testament[2]. In the case before us honour, affection, and solicitude are shown, and felt, for the departed: honour, in being borne in procession, which is performed rhythmically with a particular kind of step so that it

[1] *Op. cit.* II. 32.
[2] See the present writer's *Immortality and the Unseen World*, pp. 9, 21 f.

must be regarded as coming under the category of the
sacred dance; affection, because of the kind thought in
taking him to the spots he loved; and solicitude, in that
he is supplied with food. It is with the first of these
that we are particularly concerned just now; and here
is another illustration of it, also in India, but this time
among the Musulmans; it is not strictly speaking a
mourning rite, but it is an honorific ceremony for the
departed and may therefore be appropriately given.
During the *Muharram*[1] Festival in India one of the
ceremonies is the parading of the standard of the martyr
Qāsim. He is one of the sacred bridegrooms, for at the
age of ten he was betrothed to Fātima, daughter of
Husain, and was slain in battle. His standard is carried
by a man on horseback, who is followed by girls dancing
in his honour, and singing elegies while beating their
breasts. During another part of this festival there is the
dance of *Bharang*, or "foolish chatterer"; his whole body
is smeared with red ochre mixed with water; his head
is covered with a shawl, and a small flag is attached
to it. On his legs he carries tinkling bells, and during
his dance he cries out: "Ali, ali, ali, zang[2]!" This is all
done in honour of the departed saint. It is not a
hazardous surmise to suggest that we have here an
example of an adaptation of a rite millenniums older
than its present form; and its oldest element is, in all
probability, the sacred dance. The *Bharang*, with bells,
paint, and disguise represents a development to which
reference will be made again below.

Dances in honour of the departed are recorded of the

[1] *I.e.* "sacred," the first month of the Musulman year.
[2] Ja'far Sharif, *Islam in India, or the Qānūn-i-Islam: The
Customs of the Musulmans of India*, translated by G. A. Herklots,
pp. 161–174 (1921).

Conibos of the Ucayali river in Eastern Peru who, on
certain occasions, perform them on the graves of the
deceased[1]; also among the Maoris[2]. The inhabitants of
Dutch New Guinea dance round the images of their
departed on various festal occasions. Again, at the
funeral feast among the Gilbert islanders dancing and
singing is performed in honour of the dead; wailing is
also included in these mourning rites[3]. It is also an
important mourning rite among the Melanesians[4].
Similarly among the inhabitants of British New Guinea
a high festival is held in honour of the departed at which
a great dance takes place;

all the dancers are arranged in full dancing costume,
including heavy head-dresses of feathers, and they carry
drums and spears, sometimes also clubs and adzes. The
dance lasts the whole night[5].

In New Britain, too, the Sulka, a tribe dwelling to the
south of the Gazelle Peninsula, dance in honour of their
dead at a funeral feast[6]. An interesting account, together with an illustration, of the Maquarri dance
among the Arāwaks, one of the Indian tribes of Guiana,
is given by W. H. Brett[7]; this is danced in honour of
the departed. It is called the Maquarri dance from the

---

[1] Frazer, *GB, The Magic Art*, II. 183.
[2] J. M. Brown, *Maori and Polynesian*, p. 203. "Funeral dances
and death-bed dances are a world-wide custom. We hear of them
in Patagonia, in Abyssinia, in North America, in the East Indian
isles and in the Highlands of Scotland; we read about them in
ancient Egypt, and we can see them to-day in Spain, in Ireland,
and in the centre of France," Lilly Grove, *op. cit.* p. 4.
[3] *ERE*, IV. 434 *b*.
[4] Seligmann, *The Melanesians of British New Guinea*, pp. 358 ff.,
716 (1910).
[5] Frazer, *The Belief in Immortality*, I. 200 (1913).
[6] Frazer, *op. cit.* I. 399.
[7] *The Indian Tribes of Guiana*, pp. 154 f. (1868).

"whip," more than three feet long, which is waved about during the dance by each dancer; with it the dancers lash each other's legs until the blood flows; the whips have a sort of sacred character among the natives. It is the flowing of the blood which is now supposed to be pleasing to the dead; but it is pretty certain that this is a development; at one time the dance would have been considered as all-sufficient. Once more, among the North American Indians the funeral dance is performed at the grave when a sacrifice is made for the dead; the dancing is done round the grave and is accompanied by drum-playing and singing[1]. A similar rite is practised by the Bondas of Guinea[2], and among the aborigines of Northern Australia[3].

A case of particular interest is that of the dance of the Tami inhabitants; for while this is in honour of the dead, a further idea regarding the departed appears in connexion with it which leads on to another purpose of this mourning rite. The people of Tami, an island in the Indian archipelago, belong to the Melanesian stock; when they mourn for their dead the whole village takes part in the lamentation; the women dance death-dances in honour of the dead person while the men make preparations for the burial. Now these people, like many others, believe that when anyone has died the ghosts of his dead kinsfolk gather in the village, and are joined by the ghosts of other dead people; these ghosts may or may not be friendly inclined towards the living; but in case they are not, the people of the village take care

[1] Schoolcraft, op. cit. i. 198, 234.
[2] Featherman, Social History of the Races of Mankind, i. 413 (1881).
[3] Baldwin Spencer, The Native Tribes of the Northern Territory of Australia, pp. 234 ff. (1914).

not to leave the dancing mourners alone, they remain close at hand to help in case of need. This belief in the vicinity of the ghosts of the dead is further illustrated by these Tami islanders, for they have regular dancing seasons during which they dance round men disguised as familiar spirits; true, the dance "consists of little more than running round and round in a circle, with an occasional hop[1]," but it is essentially a dance, and its essence is more important than its form. This is a case of personating the departed in the dance; and the idea seems to be that by doing so a proof is given that the departed are really still living and that their personality is imparted, for the time being, to the dancers. Something quite similar is found among the Pulu islanders, in the Torres Straits; the performers dance in pairs, personating the deceased, for this ceremony is sometimes performed for a number of recently deceased people at once; according to Haddon

the idea evidently was to convey to the mourners the assurance that the ghost was alive, and that in the person of the dancer he visited his friends; the assurance of his life after death comforted the bereaved ones[2].

If it be asked why this personating of the deceased should be accompanied by dancing, the answer probably is that as dancing was the most usual way of honouring the departed, it would be thought of as the most efficacious means of attracting them. The Sioux, another North American Indian tribe, also performed dances at graves as a mourning rite, for they believed that in doing so they were, in some undefined way, joined by the

[1] Frazer, *op. cit.* I. 293 f.
[2] *Cambridge Anthropological Expedition to the Torres Straits,* v. 256.

departed in this dance[1]. It is very likely that the common custom of dances at funeral feasts originally had a similar object. Among the Esquimaux, for example, there are always dances at the funeral feasts, the dead are invited in song to come to the feast; offerings of food are made to them, and they feast and dance together with the living. At their great festival of the dead, which is held every few years, the dances are an important feature. The dancers dance on the graves, and on the ice if the deceased met their death by drowning[2]. Here we seem to have the purposes separately; the dancing at the funeral feasts is a joining together with the departed, the dancing on the graves is in their honour.

A very different purpose of the dance as a mourning rite next claims attention. That it sometimes has the object of appeasing the wrath of the departed, *i.e.* of their ghosts, is shown, for instance, by the fact that when among the inhabitants of Timor, an island in the East Indies, a head-hunter returns home after a successful expedition, sacrifices are offered to the man who has lost his head; and part of the ceremony consists of a dance accompanied by a song in which the death of the slain man is lamented and his forgiveness is entreated.

"Be not angry," they say, "because your head is here with us; had we been less lucky our heads might now have been exposed in your village. We have offered the sacrifice to appease you. Your spirit may now rest and leave us at peace[3]."

[1] *Die Religion in Geschichte und Gegenwart*, v. 1070.
[2] Nelson, *The Eskimo about Bering Strait*, Eighteenth Annual Report of the Bureau of Ethnology, Pt. i. 363 (1899).
[3] Frazer, *GB, Taboo and the Perils of the Soul*, p. 166.

But even among friends there are cases in which the ghost of the deceased is annoyed and has to be kept in the grave so that the surviving relatives may not be molested by it; and the dance figures as part of the ceremony. Thus, among the Arunta of Central Australia as a finale to the mourning period the people gather on the spot where the deceased died, viz. the site where he once lived and which is now burnt and deserted. Here the men and women dance round the charred remains, the men beating the air with their spears, the women doing likewise with the palms of their hands and all shouting *Wah! Wah! Wah! wa-a-ah!* This, we take it, is done to drive off both the ghost of the deceased and any evil spirits which may be lurking about the unhallowed spot. When the dancing, the description continues, which lasted about ten minutes, was over, the party proceeded to the grave at a run, the leader making a circuit from the main party, shouting wildly with a very prolonged intonation, *Ba-au! Ba-au!* The idea of the leading man making a circuit was, perhaps, though the natives could give no explanation, to prevent the spirit from doubling back to the camp from which they were supposed to be driving him.

When he reached the grave, into which the spirit of the dead man was supposed to have fled, he began dancing wildly upon it. He was soon joined by the rest of the party who began

to dance backwards and forwards on and around the grave, shouting *Wah! Wah!* and beating the air downwards as if to drive the spirit down, while with their feet they stamped upon and broke the twigs with which a newly made grave is always covered. When these were thoroughly broken up the dancing ceased[1].

[1] Spencer and Gillen, *The Native Tribes of Central Australia*, pp. 505 ff. (1899).

It must be confessed that the dancing here seems quite out of place, and yet there can be no doubt that it forms an integral part of the ceremonies. There seems to be something so entirely incongruous in scaring the ghost away by shouting at it and beating him down into his grave, and yet dancing on and around the grave which is so very frequently a mark of honour to the dead. The explanation is probably to be sought in the fact of the retention of a traditional custom concurrently with a later one which arose in consequence of the birth of new ideas regarding the activity of the spirits of the departed. We get a similar intermingling of rites among the Tarahumares of Mexico whose funeral ceremonies include the dance, though the object of the dance, in what is presumably a new form as compared with the original and traditional one, is the driving away of the ghost of the deceased. They have three funeral feasts; the first takes place a fortnight after the death, the second six months, and the last some months after that. At each of these feasts an important element is the ceremony of the *hikuli* dance. The *hikuli* is the sacred cactus, which is soaked in water and this is sprinkled over the dancers. The *hikuli* is supposed to drive away the ghost of the departed[1]. Here again the original custom of the dance performed in honour of the departed is retained, and there is added to it a further rite because in course of time new beliefs regarding the activity of the spirits of the departed had arisen; these beliefs were in reference to the possibility of anger on the part of the spirits because of their being cut off from their usual mode of life and taken away from their familiar haunts; they might be envious of those who

[1] Lumholtz, *Unknown Mexico*, i. pp. 384 ff. (1903).

were left, and might show their envy by harming the living. It became necessary, therefore, to devise means to counter these evil intentions by driving away the ghost of the departed. What these means were we know in many cases, but why particular means were chosen, such as the *hikuli*, or why they should be supposed to drive the spirit away is a matter of savage philosophy, and not always possible to penetrate. It must be evident, however, that the idea of driving away a ghost, together with the rite whereby this is effected, is subsequent in time to the simple rite of dancing in honour of the departed, because while this latter does not involve any theory as to the activity of spirits, the former obviously points to speculations on the subject. And as we have already said, the explanation of the incongruity of the two rites, as seen in the examples given, is to be sought in the retention of the earlier traditional rite concurrently with a later one which arose in consequence of the birth of new ideas regarding the activity of the spirits of the departed.

It is probable that a further step in the development of ideas regarding this activity is to be discerned in the belief that the spirit of the departed is joined by others who share with him his resentment against the living; and for safety the mourners disguise themselves, and, possibly, the dance then assumes a different purpose, namely, that of frightening the spirits away. This is said to be the purpose with which some of the tribes of Northern India dance at burials[1]; and the dance of the *Bharang*, disguised, to which reference was made above, points, perhaps, to the same thing; so also the custom of the inhabitants of the Aaru archipelago. Among them,

[1] *ERE*, iv. 481 *a*.

when a member of the family dies, all the women leave
the house with their hair hanging loose, to wail upon
the shore; they tumble over one another head over heels
in a strange kind of dance, and smear their bodies with
dirt and mud[1].

SUMMARY AND CONSIDERATIONS

Although in the Old Testament there is no mention
of dancing as a mourning or burial rite, there are strong
grounds for believing that it was practised. No customs
are more tenacious than those which are concerned with
the dead, and since some other mourning customs,
known to have been in existence among the Hebrews,
are not referred to in the Old Testament, the non-
mention of this one is no reason for supposing that it
was not practised. That the religious leaders looked
upon this, as well as various other rites performed in
connexion with the dead, as heathenish and superstitious, would of itself account for the silence of the
Old Testament on the subject. The positive grounds for
believing in its existence among the Israelites are: its
very widespread vogue among different races all over
the world; the object, or objects, for which it was performed, which involved beliefs regarding the departed
common to all races during some stages of their cultural
and religious development; and most important of all,
its existence, though in a modified form, at the present
day. Evidence is forthcoming of the rite among the
Jews in post-Christian times.

Circumambulation round a corpse, which is in the
nature of the sacred dance, was known and practised

[1] *ERE*, iv. 416 b.

among the Greeks as early as the time of Homer, who mentions it; other examples are also recorded.

The rite is in vogue among the Arabs to this day who dance in circles on their way to the place of mourning; it is performed by women and young girls.

Much evidence is forthcoming as to its practice among the Egyptians, both ancient and modern, of which various examples are given above.

Among the Greeks and Romans dancing as a mourning or burial rite was included in funeral processions and funeral games; one of the most curious customs being that of the presence of the *imagines maiorum*, or images of ancestors, in the Roman funeral processions of the nobility, who were thus believed to follow the dead body of their descendant to the grave. That a meeting between the recently deceased and his ancestors was believed to take place in the tomb we may well conceive; it would be precisely parallel to the Israelite belief expressed by the phrase of being gathered to one's fathers[1]. It was, however, during the funeral feast that dancing, in the more literal sense of the word, figured most prominently.

The sacred dance as a mourning or as a burial rite among uncivilized peoples plays an important part. Among them the objects of the rite are not only various, but contradictory; chief among these is, however, that of giving honour to the departed. A few examples, of very many, have been considered. They are taken from peoples in lands as widely spread as India, North America, South America, Central America, Australia, New Zealand, New Guinea, Guiana, the Indian archi-

---

[1] See on this the present writer's *Immortality and the Unseen World*, p. 180.

pelago, and the Torres Straits; and it would be easy to offer further instances from many other countries.

Taking these as a whole, they point indubitably to the fact that this rite was, and is, usually performed as an act of honour to the deceased. This represents, we believe, its final development, so far as intention is concerned; there are cases of its continuance in which probably no purpose could be assigned for its performance other than that of traditional use. From this point of view we shall not be far wrong in regarding the rite as a remnant of ancestor-worship; the Roman custom of carrying the *imagines maiorum* in the funeral procession is clear evidence of this. The other purposes for which it was performed betray a far less developed outlook; and the fact that they exist side by side with that of the more rational object of honouring the dead offers but another illustration of a world-wide phenomenon, to be observed even among the most civilized peoples, viz. that more or less primitive ideas can be held on some things in conjunction with advanced thought on others.

By personating the deceased in the mourning dance it is believed by some that he can be induced to return to his friends and dance with them, greatly to the comfort of the relatives. The idea is about on a level with the Roman belief in the presence of a man's ancestors, when their images are carried in the funeral procession. But the same rite can, among others, have the purpose of protecting the survivors from the spirit of the deceased; he is sometimes supposed to be annoyed at having been forcibly taken away from his familiar haunts, and lest he should vent his angry feelings on his relatives, they either dance to scare him away, or else propitiate him by various means. Another purpose of the rite is for the survivors to protect both themselves and their departed friend from the malice of other departed spirits who are believed to congregate in the vicinity of a corpse; in this case the dance is accompanied by sundry noises.

A variation of this is the dance round the corpse, whether by way of perambulation or dancing in the more literal sense. The magic circle thus formed keeps away unwelcome spirit-visitors. But this may have another purpose; it may possibly be a means of "keeping in" the spirit of the deceased, and thus preventing him from getting abroad and doing mischief. When the dance is performed round slain enemies the object of it seems to be that of propitiation.

If it be asked which of these purposes may be supposed to have been that for which the Israelites performed this rite, we imagine the reply would be: any or all of them, according to the stage of culture in which they found themselves. Two of them: that of honouring the dead, and that of forming the magic circle round the corpse (probably for keeping it safe), can be vouched for.

INDEX

224 INDEX

INDEX

225

Custom, traditional, retained
217
Cylinder seals 59
Cylix of Hieron 122
Cymbals 7, 52
Cypresses 148
Cyprus 70
— excavations in 11, 98
— inscriptions from 59 f., 72 f.,
98 f.

Dagon 47
Daḥa dances 144
Dakotahs 21, 77, 83, 101, 165 f.
— sun worship among the 77
Dālag 44, 46, 47, 48
Dance accompanied by cymbals
7
— — by hand-drums 7
— — by singing 7
— — by tambourine 121, 203
— among the Greeks 11
— — the Israelites 7
— — the natives of New Guinea
1 f.
— — the uncivilized races 8
— and music 7
— and religion 69
— applied to processions 100
— as a mourning rite among
the Greeks and Romans
207 ff.
— at funeral feasts 207
— at weddings as an initiatory
ceremony 188
— ecstatic 37 ff.
— encircling 37, 183, 199, 205
— funeral 204 ff.
— funeral, purposes of 204 ff.
— Hebrew terms for 44 ff.
— *Hikuli* 217 f.
— imitative 14
— in honour of the army of the
heavens 69
— — of the Egyptian gods 61
— in semi-circle 98
— limping 87, 111
— musical accompaniment to
51 ff.
— never useless 2
— of Jewish maidens 143

Dance of maidens in the *forum*
75
— on graves 29
— orgiastic 122
— processional 36
— represented on Greek pottery 5
— round a sacred object 88 ff.
— — altar 91 f.
— — golden calf 90
— — men disguised as familiar
spirits 214
— — slain enemies 206
— — trees 88
— — wells 88
— scaring away evil spirits 30
Dance, the dead brought back
by 30
— the dead personated in 30
Dance-spirit, the 153
Dancers sprinkled 217
Dances and funeral games 207
— at Egyptian funerals 203
— at festivals among the
Romans 149 ff.
— in celebration of victory
40 f., 159 ff.
— in honour of superhuman
powers 54 ff.
— — of the dead 205 f.
— of gods 17
— of the *Salii* 150
— performed under trees 148
Dancing accompanied by instrumental music 122
— as an act of devotion 129
— as an expression of will 6
— as a mourning rite among
savages 209 ff.
— at celebration of Eleusinian
mysteries 124
— at circumcision festivals
144 f.
— at Egyptian festivals 146
— at feasts 140 ff.
— at festivals among the Baris
153
— — — Hottentots 153 f.
— — — Kai 152
— — — Kayans 151 f.
— at Greek festivals 146 ff.

Sacred Dance, a means of a fruitful marriage 29
— — — of obtaining food 1, 4, 29, 103, 131
— — aiding the sun to run his course 27
— — among Assyrians 6
— — — Bedouin Arabs 6 f., 144
— — — Greeks 63 ff., 97 ff., 119 ff., 146 ff., 207 ff.
— — — Jews of all periods 184
— — — Romans 73 ff., 100 f., 119 ff., 149 ff.
— — — Semites 31 ff., 54 ff., 88 ff., 107 ff., 140 ff., 159 ff.
— — — uncultured races 77 ff., 101 ff., 128 ff., 151 ff., 167 ff., 184 ff., 209 ff.
— — appeasing wrath of departed 214 f.
— — as a marriage rite 1, 28 f., 41 f., 177 ff.
— — as a mourning and burial rite 29 f., 42, 194 ff.
— — assisting warriors in battle 28, 167 ff.
— — contagious 38
— — departed personated in 214
— — for magical purposes 103, 148, 151
— — ghost of deceased driven away by 217 f.
— — in honour of supernatural powers 22, 209, 218
— — in the Old Testament 8 f., 33 ff., 89, 107 ff., 140 ff.
— — introduced in Rome from Etruria 75
— — led by Theseus 70
— — many forms included under 6, 35 f.
— — objects of the 3, 19 ff.
— — origin of the 13 ff.
— — round tree 99
— — sources of information regarding the 9 ff.
— — taught by animals 18
— — unconsciousness brought about by the 25

Sacred Dance, union brought about with god by the 24, 32
Sacrifice, circuit round 94
— of pigs 102
Sacrificial victim 24
St Barbe 97
St Paul 32
Salii, the 27, 150
Sanctuaries, limping dance performed at 111
Sanctuary, circuit round 94
Sarawak, Kayans of 28, 102
Satan dancing 46
Saturn 150
Satyrs 64, 208
Saul among the prophets 109 f.
Sed festival 146
Self-laceration 38
Sennacherib 58
Sephardic Jews 198, 199 f.
— — burial of 200
Serpent worship 133
Seven circuits round a corpse 200
Sevenfold circuit 93 f.
Shabuôth 140
Shaman 128
Shiloh 142
"Showing off" 22 f.
Sicinnis 64
Sileni 208
Siloam 157
Sinaitic Peninsula, Arabs of the 95
Singers and dancers at funerals 202
Sioux, funeral dances among 214
— Indians 102
Sisera 163
Sistrum 52, 60
"Sixteen Women," the 124
Skenē 147
Speech, laudatory at burials 198
Spirit of dancing, possessed by 130
— of the departed kept in grave 216
— indwelling 16

A CATALOG OF SELECTED
DOVER BOOKS
IN ALL FIELDS OF INTEREST

A CATALOG OF SELECTED DOVER
BOOKS IN ALL FIELDS OF INTEREST

CONCERNING THE SPIRITUAL IN ART, Wassily Kandinsky. Pioneering work by father of abstract art. Thoughts on color theory, nature of art. Analysis of earlier masters. 12 illustrations. 80pp. of text. 5⅜ x 8½. 23411-8

ANIMALS: 1,419 Copyright-Free Illustrations of Mammals, Birds, Fish, Insects, etc., Jim Harter (ed.). Clear wood engravings present, in extremely lifelike poses, over 1,000 species of animals. One of the most extensive pictorial sourcebooks of its kind. Captions. Index. 284pp. 9 x 12. 23766-4

CELTIC ART: The Methods of Construction, George Bain. Simple geometric techniques for making Celtic interlacements, spirals, Kells-type initials, animals, humans, etc. Over 500 illustrations. 160pp. 9 x 12. (Available in U.S. only.) 22923-8

AN ATLAS OF ANATOMY FOR ARTISTS, Fritz Schider. Most thorough reference work on art anatomy in the world. Hundreds of illustrations, including selections from works by Vesalius, Leonardo, Goya, Ingres, Michelangelo, others. 593 illustrations. 192pp. 7⅛ x 10¼. 20241-0

CELTIC HAND STROKE-BY-STROKE (Irish Half-Uncial from "The Book of Kells"): An Arthur Baker Calligraphy Manual, Arthur Baker. Complete guide to creating each letter of the alphabet in distinctive Celtic manner. Covers hand position, strokes, pens, inks, paper, more. Illustrated. 48pp. 8¼ x 11. 24336-2

EASY ORIGAMI, John Montroll. Charming collection of 32 projects (hat, cup, pelican, piano, swan, many more) specially designed for the novice origami hobbyist. Clearly illustrated easy-to-follow instructions insure that even beginning papercrafters will achieve successful results. 48pp. 8¼ x 11. 27298-2

THE COMPLETE BOOK OF BIRDHOUSE CONSTRUCTION FOR WOODWORKERS, Scott D. Campbell. Detailed instructions, illustrations, tables. Also data on bird habitat and instinct patterns. Bibliography. 3 tables. 63 illustrations in 15 figures. 48pp. 5¼ x 8½. 24407-5

BLOOMINGDALE'S ILLUSTRATED 1886 CATALOG: Fashions, Dry Goods and Housewares, Bloomingdale Brothers. Famed merchants' extremely rare catalog depicting about 1,700 products: clothing, housewares, firearms, dry goods, jewelry, more. Invaluable for dating, identifying vintage items. Also, copyright-free graphics for artists, designers. Co-published with Henry Ford Museum & Greenfield Village. 160pp. 8¼ x 11. 25780-0

HISTORIC COSTUME IN PICTURES, Braun & Schneider. Over 1,450 costumed figures in clearly detailed engravings–from dawn of civilization to end of 19th century. Captions. Many folk costumes. 256pp. 8⅜ x 11¾. 23150-X

PERSPECTIVE FOR ARTISTS, Rex Vicat Cole. Depth, perspective of sky and sea, shadows, much more, not usually covered. 391 diagrams, 81 reproductions of drawings and paintings. 279pp. 5⅜ x 8½. 22487-2

DRAWING THE LIVING FIGURE, Joseph Sheppard. Innovative approach to artistic anatomy focuses on specifics of surface anatomy, rather than muscles and bones. Over 170 drawings of live models in front, back and side views, and in widely varying poses. Accompanying diagrams. 177 illustrations. Introduction. Index. 144pp. 8⅜ x11¼. 26723-7

GOTHIC AND OLD ENGLISH ALPHABETS: 100 Complete Fonts, Dan X. Solo. Add power, elegance to posters, signs, other graphics with 100 stunning copyright-free alphabets: Blackstone, Dolbey, Germania, 97 more—including many lower-case, numerals, punctuation marks. 104pp. 8⅛ x 11. 24695-7

HOW TO DO BEADWORK, Mary White. Fundamental book on craft from simple projects to five-bead chains and woven works. 106 illustrations. 142pp. 5⅜ x 8. 20697-1

THE BOOK OF WOOD CARVING, Charles Marshall Sayers. Finest book for beginners discusses fundamentals and offers 34 designs. "Absolutely first rate . . . well thought out and well executed."–E. J. Tangerman. 118pp. 7¾ x 10⅝. 23654-4

ILLUSTRATED CATALOG OF CIVIL WAR MILITARY GOODS: Union Army Weapons, Insignia, Uniform Accessories, and Other Equipment, Schuyler, Hartley, and Graham. Rare, profusely illustrated 1846 catalog includes Union Army uniform and dress regulations, arms and ammunition, coats, insignia, flags, swords, rifles, etc. 226 illustrations. 160pp. 9 x 12. 24939-5

WOMEN'S FASHIONS OF THE EARLY 1900s: An Unabridged Republication of "New York Fashions, 1909," National Cloak & Suit Co. Rare catalog of mail-order fashions documents women's and children's clothing styles shortly after the turn of the century. Captions offer full descriptions, prices. Invaluable resource for fashion, costume historians. Approximately 725 illustrations. 128pp. 8⅜ x 11¼. 27276-1

THE 1912 AND 1915 GUSTAV STICKLEY FURNITURE CATALOGS, Gustav Stickley. With over 200 detailed illustrations and descriptions, these two catalogs are essential reading and reference materials and identification guides for Stickley furniture. Captions cite materials, dimensions and prices. 112pp. 6½ x 9¼. 26676-1

EARLY AMERICAN LOCOMOTIVES, John H. White, Jr. Finest locomotive engravings from early 19th century: historical (1804–74), main-line (after 1870), special, foreign, etc. 147 plates. 142pp. 11⅜ x 8¼. 22772-3

THE TALL SHIPS OF TODAY IN PHOTOGRAPHS, Frank O. Braynard. Lavishly illustrated tribute to nearly 100 majestic contemporary sailing vessels: Amerigo Vespucci, Clearwater, Constitution, Eagle, Mayflower, Sea Cloud, Victory, many more. Authoritative captions provide statistics, background on each ship. 190 black-and-white photographs and illustrations. Introduction. 128pp. 8⅞ x 11¾. 27163-3

CATALOG OF DOVER BOOKS

LITTLE BOOK OF EARLY AMERICAN CRAFTS AND TRADES, Peter Stockham (ed.). 1807 children's book explains crafts and trades: baker, hatter, cooper, potter, and many others. 23 copperplate illustrations. 140pp. 4⅝ x 6. 23336-7

VICTORIAN FASHIONS AND COSTUMES FROM HARPER'S BAZAR, 1867–1898, Stella Blum (ed.). Day costumes, evening wear, sports clothes, shoes, hats, other accessories in over 1,000 detailed engravings. 320pp. 9⅜ x 12¼. 22990-4

GUSTAV STICKLEY, THE CRAFTSMAN, Mary Ann Smith. Superb study surveys broad scope of Stickley's achievement, especially in architecture. Design philosophy, rise and fall of the Craftsman empire, descriptions and floor plans for many Craftsman houses, more. 86 black-and-white halftones. 31 line illustrations. Introduction 208pp. 6½ x 9¼. 27210-9

THE LONG ISLAND RAIL ROAD IN EARLY PHOTOGRAPHS, Ron Ziel. Over 220 rare photos, informative text document origin (1844) and development of rail service on Long Island. Vintage views of early trains, locomotives, stations, passengers, crews, much more. Captions. 8⅞ x 11¾. 26301-0

VOYAGE OF THE LIBERDADE, Joshua Slocum. Great 19th-century mariner's thrilling, first-hand account of the wreck of his ship off South America, the 35-foot boat he built from the wreckage, and its remarkable voyage home. 128pp. 5⅜ x 8½. 40022-0

TEN BOOKS ON ARCHITECTURE, Vitruvius. The most important book ever written on architecture. Early Roman aesthetics, technology, classical orders, site selection, all other aspects. Morgan translation. 331pp. 5⅜ x 8½. 20645-9

THE HUMAN FIGURE IN MOTION, Eadweard Muybridge. More than 4,500 stopped-action photos, in action series, showing undraped men, women, children jumping, lying down, throwing, sitting, wrestling, carrying, etc. 390pp. 7⅞ x 10⅝. 20204-6 Clothbd.

TREES OF THE EASTERN AND CENTRAL UNITED STATES AND CANADA, William M. Harlow. Best one-volume guide to 140 trees. Full descriptions, woodlore, range, etc. Over 600 illustrations. Handy size. 288pp. 4½ x 6⅜. 20395-6

SONGS OF WESTERN BIRDS, Dr. Donald J. Borror. Complete song and call repertoire of 60 western species, including flycatchers, juncoes, cactus wrens, many more–includes fully illustrated booklet. Cassette and manual 99913-0

GROWING AND USING HERBS AND SPICES, Milo Miloradovich. Versatile handbook provides all the information needed for cultivation and use of all the herbs and spices available in North America. 4 illustrations. Index. Glossary. 236pp. 5⅜ x 8½. 25058-X

BIG BOOK OF MAZES AND LABYRINTHS, Walter Shepherd. 50 mazes and labyrinths in all–classical, solid, ripple, and more–in one great volume. Perfect inexpensive puzzler for clever youngsters. Full solutions. 112pp. 8⅛ x 11. 22951-3

CATALOG OF DOVER BOOKS

PIANO TUNING, J. Cree Fischer. Clearest, best book for beginner, amateur. Simple repairs, raising dropped notes, tuning by easy method of flattened fifths. No previous skills needed. 4 illustrations. 201pp. 5⅜ x 8½. 23267-0

HINTS TO SINGERS, Lillian Nordica. Selecting the right teacher, developing confidence, overcoming stage fright, and many other important skills receive thoughtful discussion in this indispensible guide, written by a world-famous diva of four decades' experience. 96pp. 5⅜ x 8½. 40094-8

THE COMPLETE NONSENSE OF EDWARD LEAR, Edward Lear. All nonsense limericks, zany alphabets, Owl and Pussycat, songs, nonsense botany, etc., illustrated by Lear. Total of 320pp. 5⅜ x 8½. (Available in U.S. only.) 20167-8

VICTORIAN PARLOUR POETRY: An Annotated Anthology, Michael R. Turner. 117 gems by Longfellow, Tennyson, Browning, many lesser-known poets. "The Village Blacksmith," "Curfew Must Not Ring Tonight," "Only a Baby Small," dozens more, often difficult to find elsewhere. Index of poets, titles, first lines. xxiii + 325pp. 5⅜ x 8¼. 27044-0

DUBLINERS, James Joyce. Fifteen stories offer vivid, tightly focused observations of the lives of Dublin's poorer classes. At least one, "The Dead," is considered a masterpiece. Reprinted complete and unabridged from standard edition. 160pp. 5³⁄₁₆ x 8¼. 26870-5

GREAT WEIRD TALES: 14 Stories by Lovecraft, Blackwood, Machen and Others, S. T. Joshi (ed.). 14 spellbinding tales, including "The Sin Eater," by Fiona McLeod, "The Eye Above the Mantel," by Frank Belknap Long, as well as renowned works by R. H. Barlow, Lord Dunsany, Arthur Machen, W. C. Morrow and eight other masters of the genre. 256pp. 5⅜ x 8½. (Available in U.S. only.) 40436-6

THE BOOK OF THE SACRED MAGIC OF ABRAMELIN THE MAGE, translated by S. MacGregor Mathers. Medieval manuscript of ceremonial magic. Basic document in Aleister Crowley, Golden Dawn groups. 268pp. 5⅜ x 8½. 23211-5

NEW RUSSIAN-ENGLISH AND ENGLISH-RUSSIAN DICTIONARY, M. A. O'Brien. This is a remarkably handy Russian dictionary, containing a surprising amount of information, including over 70,000 entries. 366pp. 4½ x 6⅛. 20208-9

HISTORIC HOMES OF THE AMERICAN PRESIDENTS, Second, Revised Edition, Irvin Haas. A traveler's guide to American Presidential homes, most open to the public, depicting and describing homes occupied by every American President from George Washington to George Bush. With visiting hours, admission charges, travel routes. 175 photographs. Index. 160pp. 8¼ x 11. 26751-2

NEW YORK IN THE FORTIES, Andreas Feininger. 162 brilliant photographs by the well-known photographer, formerly with *Life* magazine. Commuters, shoppers, Times Square at night, much else from city at its peak. Captions by John von Hartz. 181pp. 9¼ x 10¾. 23585-8

INDIAN SIGN LANGUAGE, William Tomkins. Over 525 signs developed by Sioux and other tribes. Written instructions and diagrams. Also 290 pictographs. 111pp. 6⅛ x 9¼. 22029-X

CATALOG OF DOVER BOOKS

ANATOMY: A Complete Guide for Artists, Joseph Sheppard. A master of figure drawing shows artists how to render human anatomy convincingly. Over 460 illustrations. 224pp. 8⅜ x 11¼. 27279-6

MEDIEVAL CALLIGRAPHY: Its History and Technique, Marc Drogin. Spirited history, comprehensive instruction manual covers 13 styles (ca. 4th century through 15th). Excellent photographs; directions for duplicating medieval techniques with modern tools. 224pp. 8⅜ x 11¼. 26142-5

DRIED FLOWERS: How to Prepare Them, Sarah Whitlock and Martha Rankin. Complete instructions on how to use silica gel, meal and borax, perlite aggregate, sand and borax, glycerine and water to create attractive permanent flower arrangements. 12 illustrations. 32pp. 5⅜ x 8½. 21802-3

EASY-TO-MAKE BIRD FEEDERS FOR WOODWORKERS, Scott D. Campbell. Detailed, simple-to-use guide for designing, constructing, caring for and using feeders. Text, illustrations for 12 classic and contemporary designs. 96pp. 5⅜ x 8½. 25847-5

SCOTTISH WONDER TALES FROM MYTH AND LEGEND, Donald A. Mackenzie. 16 lively tales tell of giants rumbling down mountainsides, of a magic wand that turns stone pillars into warriors, of gods and goddesses, evil hags, powerful forces and more. 240pp. 5⅜ x 8½. 29677-6

THE HISTORY OF UNDERCLOTHES, C. Willett Cunnington and Phyllis Cunnington. Fascinating, well-documented survey covering six centuries of English undergarments, enhanced with over 100 illustrations: 12th-century laced-up bodice, footed long drawers (1795), 19th-century bustles, 19th-century corsets for men, Victorian "bust improvers," much more. 272pp. 5⅜ x 8¼. 27124-2

ARTS AND CRAFTS FURNITURE: The Complete Brooks Catalog of 1912, Brooks Manufacturing Co. Photos and detailed descriptions of more than 150 now very collectible furniture designs from the Arts and Crafts movement depict davenports, settees, buffets, desks, tables, chairs, bedsteads, dressers and more, all built of solid, quarter-sawed oak. Invaluable for students and enthusiasts of antiques, Americana and the decorative arts. 80pp. 6½ x 9¼. 27471-3

WILBUR AND ORVILLE: A Biography of the Wright Brothers, Fred Howard. Definitive, crisply written study tells the full story of the brothers' lives and work. A vividly written biography, unparalleled in scope and color, that also captures the spirit of an extraordinary era. 560pp. 6⅛ x 9¼. 40297-5

THE ARTS OF THE SAILOR: Knotting, Splicing and Ropework, Hervey Garrett Smith. Indispensable shipboard reference covers tools, basic knots and useful hitches; handsewing and canvas work, more. Over 100 illustrations. Delightful reading for sea lovers. 256pp. 5⅜ x 8½. 26440-8

FRANK LLOYD WRIGHT'S FALLINGWATER: The House and Its History, Second, Revised Edition, Donald Hoffmann. A total revision—both in text and illustrations—of the standard document on Fallingwater, the boldest, most personal architectural statement of Wright's mature years, updated with valuable new material from the recently opened Frank Lloyd Wright Archives. "Fascinating"—*The New York Times.* 116 illustrations. 128pp. 9¼ x 10¾. 27430-6

CATALOG OF DOVER BOOKS

THE STORY OF THE TITANIC AS TOLD BY ITS SURVIVORS, Jack Winocour (ed.). What it was really like. Panic, despair, shocking inefficiency, and a little heroism. More thrilling than any fictional account. 26 illustrations. 320pp. 5⅜ x 8½.
20610-6

FAIRY AND FOLK TALES OF THE IRISH PEASANTRY, William Butler Yeats (ed.). Treasury of 64 tales from the twilight world of Celtic myth and legend: "The Soul Cages," "The Kildare Pooka," "King O'Toole and his Goose," many more. Introduction and Notes by W. B. Yeats. 352pp. 5⅜ x 8½.
26941-8

BUDDHIST MAHAYANA TEXTS, E. B. Cowell and others (eds.). Superb, accurate translations of basic documents in Mahayana Buddhism, highly important in history of religions. The Buddha-karita of Asvaghosha, Larger Sukhavativyuha, more. 448pp. 5⅜ x 8½.
25552-2

ONE TWO THREE . . . INFINITY: Facts and Speculations of Science, George Gamow. Great physicist's fascinating, readable overview of contemporary science: number theory, relativity, fourth dimension, entropy, genes, atomic structure, much more. 128 illustrations. Index. 352pp. 5⅜ x 8½.
25664-2

EXPERIMENTATION AND MEASUREMENT, W. J. Youden. Introductory manual explains laws of measurement in simple terms and offers tips for achieving accuracy and minimizing errors. Mathematics of measurement, use of instruments, experimenting with machines. 1994 edition. Foreword. Preface. Introduction. Epilogue. Selected Readings. Glossary. Index. Tables and figures. 128pp. 5⅜ x 8½.   40451-X

DALÍ ON MODERN ART: The Cuckolds of Antiquated Modern Art, Salvador Dalí. Influential painter skewers modern art and its practitioners. Outrageous evaluations of Picasso, Cézanne, Turner, more. 15 renderings of paintings discussed. 44 calligraphic decorations by Dalí. 96pp. 5⅜ x 8½. (Available in U.S. only.)
29220-7

ANTIQUE PLAYING CARDS: A Pictorial History, Henry René D'Allemagne. Over 900 elaborate, decorative images from rare playing cards (14th–20th centuries): Bacchus, death, dancing dogs, hunting scenes, royal coats of arms, players cheating, much more. 96pp. 9¼ x 12¼.
29265-7

MAKING FURNITURE MASTERPIECES: 30 Projects with Measured Drawings, Franklin H. Gottshall. Step-by-step instructions, illustrations for constructing handsome, useful pieces, among them a Sheraton desk, Chippendale chair, Spanish desk, Queen Anne table and a William and Mary dressing mirror. 224pp. 8⅛ x 11¼.
29338-6

THE FOSSIL BOOK: A Record of Prehistoric Life, Patricia V. Rich et al. Profusely illustrated definitive guide covers everything from single-celled organisms and dinosaurs to birds and mammals and the interplay between climate and man. Over 1,500 illustrations. 760pp. 7½ x 10⅛.
29371-8

Paperbound unless otherwise indicated. Available at your book dealer, online at **www.doverpublications.com**, or by writing to Dept. GI, Dover Publications, Inc., 31 East 2nd Street, Mineola, NY 11501. For current price information or for free catalogues (please indicate field of interest), write to Dover Publications or log on to **www.doverpublications.com** and see every Dover book in print. Dover publishes more than 500 books each year on science, elementary and advanced mathematics, biology, music, art, literary history, social sciences, and other areas.